Race Against Time

WITHDRAWN

Helder Camara

translated by Della Couling

Sheed and Ward · London and Sydney

First published 1971
Sheed and Ward Ltd, 33 Maiden Lane, London WC2E 7LA, and
Sheed and Ward Pty Ltd, 204 Clarence Street, Sydney NSW 2000
Originally published as *Pour Arriver A Temps*, Desclée de Brouwer,
Brussels 1970
© Sheed and Ward Ltd 1971

Nihil obstat : J M T Barton *Censor*
Imprimatur : +Victor Guazelli *Vicar General*
Westminster, 3 March 1971

ISBN : 0 7220 0627 6
This book is set in 11/13 Linotype Times
Made and printed in Great Britain by
William Clowes & Sons Limited, London, Beccles and Colchester

Contents

Preface

In these pages you will encounter some ideas which will recur time and time again, approached from different angles, according to circumstances. Here is everything I prize, always dreaming, always hoping, striving every day to love more.

I hunger and thirst for peace. For that peace of Christ which rests on justice. I hunger and thirst for dialogue and this is why I hurry wherever I am beckoned, in search of what can bring men together in the name of the essential.

If one country has not heard my appeal, tomorrow perhaps another one will. If one institution refuses to reply—or cannot—perhaps another is there, waiting. This is why I cannot rest. If the hour of Providence has not yet sounded, it may be soon.

What am I? Naive? Presumptuous? Or an agitator? Christ, my only Judge, knows the answer. I seek only one thing: to follow more faithfully every day the Pilgrim of Peace, and to speak in the name of those who are hindered from so doing.

My plan, I am well aware, may call to mind the

combat against Goliath. But the hand of God was with the young shepherd and David conquered the Philistine, with his faith, a sling and five small stones.

H.C.

Part 1

The refusal

1
Injustice on a world scale

Address to a conference on 'The Church and the World', Montreal, May 1968

There is one fact whose gravity, I fervently hope, you are already aware of: the fact of the gap, daily growing wider and deeper, between the wealthy countries and the poor countries.

Before suggesting a global strategy for our churches of the Americas—Latin American and North American—allow me to point out some serious consequences of this gap.

In Latin America, there is a temptation to radical action and violence, given the obvious practical impossibility of passing from the spiral of underdevelopment to that of development. This temptation is serious especially because we know that the super-comfort of the 'haves', who are becoming ever less numerous, is paid for by the misery of the mass of 'have-nots', who are becoming more and more numerous. This temptation is the more serious because there are powerful people in our countries who, to safeguard their own prestige and their wealth, become the allies, or even the collaborators and henchmen, of those who are exploiting us.

In North America, broadly speaking (United States and Canada), there is also a temptation to radical action and violence. I hope I may be forgiven for my presumption in mentioning very delicate and intimate problems: I do not feel foreign in any country of the world; I am only a human voice, a human conscience.

Canada then, like the United States, finds itself among the four, five or six countries of the world which, in a few years, will stand every chance of becoming post-industrialised countries, way ahead even of the highly industrialised countries, and quite out of sight of the pre-industrialised countries.

And yet there are thirty million North Americans in a situation unworthy of the human condition; there is, as you know better than anyone else, a poor Canada within a rich Canada.

And I am not only thinking of Northern Canada, that frozen waste and challenge to the technology of tomorrow. I am thinking of the Canada which is only too aware of the presence of a too-powerful neighbour: of the Canada suffering the consequences of a sort of internal colonialism. . . . Obviously, problems of this size create a climate which, sooner or later, leads or will lead to radical action and violence.

The church in the Americas
Please remember that my position as a bishop does not bring me any special competence, given the fact that hunger and thirst for justice and peace lead me to approach subjects far removed from dogmas—subjects in which I am by no means an expert.

Allow me to summarise my thought in the ten following propositions:

1. *Three hundred years late*

The church, in Latin America at least, needs to revise its triumphalist outlook—it has sins of omission to expiate.

Looking at the world, we used to have the impression that there was, within humanity, a christian continent, *the* christian continent: Latin America, the creation of the church and a reservoir of christianity for the rest of the world.

Today we are coming to see things more humbly and more realistically: if christianity is the great spiritual force of the continent, we have our share of responsibility for the situation of America. What have we done to hinder a very small group of privileged people from amassing wealth at the expense of the poverty of the masses? What have we done to hinder millions of sons of God from falling into a sub-human condition in a sub-human life?

If, today, we sometimes give an impression of eagerness, it is because in Latin America we christians are already more than three hundred years late....

2. *A magical christianity*

We must rise above the magical and fatalist christianity which we have passed on to the Latin American masses.

In practice we have justified Marx by celebrating mass on the estates of the great landowners for the African slaves of yesterday and for the national slaves of today (the so-called free workers, living in a condition of bondage).

Religion proclaimed to men without freedom necessarily becomes a magical and fatalist religion: the will of God must be accepted (including the phenomena of nature that man has the right and the duty to fight and conquer, and including all the injustices of men). The only real hope left is heaven: a hope for aid in the hour of affliction: a final hope, after the sufferings of this earth.

How can the Latin-American masses be led to a religious practice which transcends these shameful travesties? The changes to be undertaken are so profound that we shall need great skill and a rare psychological sense. We must go to the masses and learn to speak their language. We must reaffirm our faith in the Creator and Father, who has complete power to intervene in creation. But we must demonstrate that God himself wished man to be capable of dominating nature and completing creation. We must teach straightforwardly that social injustices are a problem to be faced today. (The masses say: 'Some are born rich, some are born poor. We must accept the will of God.')

It is thrilling to try to live and make live, not a new christianity—there is only one Christ and he suffices for us!—it is thrilling to try to live and make live authentic christianity, the christianity of all ages that our human weakness so often manages to forget or distort.

3. *Challenging the rich*

We must speak more clearly and more loudly to the rich and the governments of our countries.

It is very difficult to get rid of one's own privileges. In the Gospel, Christ spoke of the danger of wealth. When there is talk of basic reforms, the possessing classes in our countries feel attacked and imagine sinister preparations for assault and robbery.

In theory, governments understand the necessity for profound and rapid changes; in practice, they think of their duty to safeguard the established order, without asking themselves whether it really is order and not generalised disorder.

Young people, more logical and more courageous than our generation, when faced with the establishment and the passivity of the 'haves', and with the weakness of governments, get the impression that only violence will be capable of shaking these structures.

We must speak more directly, more clearly and more forcefully to the propertied classes and to the men in government.

4. *Non-violence*

We must find legitimate and democratic pressures.

Three main reasons lead us to attempt a non-violent action, understood as legitimate and democratic pressure:

—An effective action which is peaceful, dynamic and active, courageous in the hope of snatching from violence those, especially the young, whose patience has reached breaking-point;

—human weakness must be helped: for without legitimate and democratic pressures, neither the propertied classes nor the governments will shift;

—if we are not in favour of violence, we must resort

7

to non-violent action in order not to hover helplessly in space.

Latin America is beginning an experiment of non-violent action on a continental scale, with the plan for commemorating the anniversary of the Declaration of Human Rights.

Non-violence is not at all the same as passivity and lack of courage. On the contrary: within the strict limits of democratic methods, with respect for truth, justice and love, we shall quickly become inconvenient. We shall be there to denounce suppression or mockery of basic rights, to demand that they be respected. . . .

Now that the means of social communication are slipping out of our control, when aid, favours, and attention are going into eclipse, your understanding and your help will be of use to us, especially as an echo from outside.

5. *The school*

The special sector of our responsibility are the schools which belong to us: apart from a few exceptions, we have not accepted the children of the workers nor have we made good use of having side by side the children of the middle class and those of the rich.

Always safeguarding the 'elites', we have been prisoners of Greco-Latin humanism and we have not accepted and understood scientific humanism. Education, in our hands, very often functioned as an alien and alienating force. In this sense, we have our share of responsibility for the technological backwardness of Latin America.

We also have a share of responsibility for the failure

of the schools to be a force for human development. We have not been sufficiently touched by the truths at the heart of the christian message which can help the masses to become a people, to reach a human standard of living, to have a reason for living, or by the truths capable of opening the eyes, the minds, and the hearts of the rich, and giving them a new and authentic hierarchy of values.

Today when the state is tending to extend schooling, endeavouring to render it accessible to all, today, when the state is preoccupied with technological training, let us have the intelligence not to combat a concrete and definite orientation, because we feel ourselves attacked in our traditional role of defenders of the private school.

Perhaps if we are freed from the immediate responsibilities of secondary and university education, we shall be freer to work in the fields of basic education and of popular culture.

6. *Justice between the two worlds*

The social revolution necessary in Latin America presupposes and demands a social revolution in North America.

If even Canada submits in some areas to the influence of the United States, you will easily understand why the third world keeps vital links with the developed world, both capitalist and socialist regimes.

The selling prices of our raw materials are imposed on us without appeal, and they become daily less favourable to us; the prices of manufactured goods are imposed on us without appeal, and they become daily more inaccessible.

Foreign investments in our country, when they are repatriated, illegally return incredible interest rates. If the third world demands a fundamental examination of this problem—at Geneva and subsequently at New Delhi—the developed world, too sure of itself, doesn't find the matter worth attention.

Our raw materials themselves will become daily less necessary, thanks to the development of synthetic substitutes. And the gap between the developed world and the underdeveloped world? The rich countries dictate the recipe to us: we must have the courage to embark on massive family planning programmes; we must be sober, honest and hard-working. . . .

We shall have the courage to achieve a responsible parenthood without falling into the exaggeration of reducing the whole delicate problem of development to birth-control alone. We shall have the courage to be demanding towards the moneyed classes and governments of our countries. But the rich countries must not become blind and deaf, blockaded in their own egoism: it is far from sufficient to indulge in philanthropy and throw a few crumbs to the poor of the third world. There is a problem of justice in the relations between our two worlds: the developed and the under-developed.

7. *A human revolution*

What convictions should be created in the man in the street? In the developed world, the problems of the relations between the wealthy countries and the poor countries must come to be seen in a totally different way: in such a way that even the average man, the man in the street, can understand that it is by no means enough for Canada (and the whole developed world) to give 1% of its gross national product to Latin America (and the rest of the underdeveloped world). Much more than increasing this percentage, we have to revise fundamentally international policies on trade, industry, agriculture, finance, labour.... We have to achieve a new hierarchy of values, a human revolution.

8. *To believe in justice and love*

If we do not believe in the power of justice, truth and love, if we do not believe in the power of ideas and in democratic methods, then it is useless to keep open the churches, the universities, the communications media and parliament.

But we believe in all this.

Then, if there is an ever-increasing danger for the peace of the world, given the fact that without justice we shall not have peace and that injustice exists on a world scale—why not mobilise the universities to investigate the complex problems involved in the relations between the developed world and the underdeveloped world? Why not mobilise the leaders of all the religions, all those interested in the peace of the world? Why not mobilise politicians, the business leaders, workers' leaders and the mass media?

9. *True collaboration*

What practical steps can we take?

Should public or private aid, in money, be maintained or ended? As profound changes demand time, aid can and must be maintained, as long as there are specific projects, conducted by honest and efficient people.

Should public and private aid, in personnel, be maintained or ended? Aid in the form of personnel can and should be maintained if, on the Latin American side, there are worthwhile projects to employ them; and if on the North American side there are candidates capable of imitating the Incarnation of the Word (in their capacity for emptying themselves by forgetting a richer culture, and taking on themselves a poorer culture).

But true aid, true collaboration on the part of the church in North America, would be to employ all the moral force at its command to lead the United States and Canada (Europe would follow automatically) to a fundamental revision of the relations between the developed world and the underdeveloped world.

Has the church the power to lead the universities— even its own—to examine in depth the reports of the first and the second UNCTAD?[1] If this is not done, if we base ourselves on errors, then we would be aiding the third world by demonstrating the weakness of its position; but if this is done, if we base ourselves on the true situation, then it becomes serious because it is a matter—we wish to repeat—of injustice on a world scale. And without justice, peace is impossible.

Has the church the means to promote a meeting of leaders of all the main religions, certainly of all those interested in peace, which demands a concern for justice?

Here again, it would be necessary to call attention to the views of the third world, expressed, for example, in the Algiers Charter.

[1] United Nations Conference on Trade and Development, first session Geneva, 1964, second session New Delhi, 1968.

The church could encourage similar meetings with the same objectives: meetings of business leaders; meetings of workers' leaders; meetings of politicians. . . .

These different meetings would be events of interest and the communications media would be there, giving a world-wide echo to the studies and discussions. . . .

10. *The true policy*

Why was a meeting of the American hierarchies held in Washington at the beginning of Pope John's pontificate, with six bishops from the United States, six bishops from Canada and six bishops from Latin America? The meeting had been suggested to Pope Pius XII, who immediately gave the idea his blessing but died before it took place. What was the real reason for the Latin Americans' wish for a dialogue with North America? They were asking for understanding, much more than for money or personnel.

They wanted to make, together, fraternally, an effort to make the whole continent aware, and confront people with the true picture of the relations between the developed world and the underdeveloped world.

With the best of intentions, individuals and developed countries, wishing to be practical and objective, have tended to think only of aid in terms of money and sending clergy, nuns and laymen. But, in these solutions, the essential element was lacking. . . . Subsequently, CICOP has made efforts to go back to the beginning, in the sense of rediscovering and recapturing the real intention of the meeting of the hierarchies.

Canada can help, however, to take another decisive step: through its universities and institutes, it can help to revise fundamentally policies on trade, industry, agriculture, finance, labour. I want to emphasise the point: our task is to attain a new hierarchy of values, a human revolution.

Perhaps you will feel a little uneasy in appearing to invade political territory. Remember that this is not an issue of partisan politics; it is the common good which is at stake. You will be helping to free the world of an injustice on a world scale. You will therefore be working directly for a world peace.

2
The scandal of sub-men

Closing speech to the 6th International Annual Conference of the Catholic Inter-American Cooperation Programme, New York, January 1969

Why is it that the fundamental human rights, which everyone greets with enthusiasm and emotion, are so difficult to respect in practice?

Theoretically one would think that if these really are human rights, all men and all governments would feel a real eagerness to respect them fully. It turns out that it is easy, very easy, for everyone to want his own rights respected, but it is difficult, and sometimes indeed very difficult, to respect the rights of others.

Is there hope for human rights?

Everyone knows that even the UN which, twenty years ago, experienced the wonderful moment of the declaration of Human Rights, still lacks the moral force to proclaim even Article No. 1? How can we say that 'all men are born free and equal in dignity and in rights' if, within the UN itself, the member states are

15

not equal in dignity and in rights? As long as there are strong states and weak states within the UN:

—The Declaration of Human Rights will only be fine-sounding phrases, empty promises;

—The Declaration will have no power to do anything effective for the full development of the individual man and the equal progress of humanity;

—The Declaration will be a sham; the super-powers will carry on with the arms race and militarily oriented space programmes, with more and more inhuman wars, economic blockades, and the pretence of aid side by side with de facto proletarisation on a world scale.

Perhaps, after all, it would in effect be preferable for the UN to maintain its discrimination between states with or without a vote: it would be one piece of hypocrisy less. The strong states will never in practice allow their interests to be sacrificed: they will not do so for the very simple reason that not even the weakest states will allow themselves to be frustrated in what they see as their essential interests.

As long as law has to rely on force to be respected, international organisations will waste vast amounts of money and patience—only to obtain victories which may appear admirable but are really only a drop in the ocean; they will fail whenever they run up against the interests of the super-powers.

Giving the UN a military superiority over any one of the super-powers taken on its own is a dream: the UN will always depend for arms largely on the super-powers. This course would simply put the UN in the arms race.

To wait for the super-powers of today to decline—as all the great empires of yesterday grew and collapsed in their turn—is to forget that the super-powers of today will only see their own decline as the super-powers of tomorrow begin to assert themselves.

Does this introduction betray an essential pessimism about human rights? Is it worth while to uphold the rights of man in the hope that they are valid as an ideal to be progressively attained?

If the moral forces of the entire world were in agreement on human rights and combined to exercise, with political realism, a liberating moral pressure within their respective countries, perhaps the impossible would be accomplished.

First of all, we should have to see whether the moral forces can be mobilised, or to what degree they are compromised. I rely in this on your sympathy, tempered by realism.

Keep in mind that throughout the centuries, humanity has been led by daring minorities: the ideal would be that, in place of daring, they had lucidity and good sense.

When I refer to the moral forces which I think can be mobilised, always remember that it is not a matter of obtaining unanimity within each, nor even a majority; but a lucid and daring minority.

Have you ever thought what it would mean for the real implementation of the Rights of Man to have a pact between the lucid and daring minorities in the different religions of the world, in the universities of all countries, in the news media, among the working class and managements, in the world of technology, among politicians and soldiers?

In order not to leave you with an impression of pure fantasy, let me give some content to this vague and apparently wild suggestion. I shall even try to outline what our immediate aims ought to be, in the USA and Latin America.

The impasse

Fraternal suggestions to North Americans

Get your universities to prepare evidence demonstrating the total folly, the collective suicide a new world war would represent, and also the incredible losses in human lives, in money and in prestige that local wars, of the Vietnam type, represent.

At the same time, get your universities to prepare material showing how it is quite possible for all men on earth to raise themselves to a level compatible with human dignity.

With such material, which it is perfectly possible to prepare, the Pentagon could formulate its strategy against war: if development is the new name for peace, under-development, poverty, is the new name for war.

Imagine the effect on the world of the reformulation by the Pentagon of an idea of social order which is not confused with disorder and generalised injustice; of an idea of national and continental security, based on the principle that poverty reduces men to slavery and is an agent of trouble and revolt, and not forgetting that on a world plane humanity is rapidly approaching a clash between a smaller and smaller but more and more powerful minority and almost the whole of mankind reduced to despair.

You could all take up, this time once and for all, the war against poverty within your own country. This

18

would be your point of honour, to assure fully the rights of man to all those—white and black—who shelter beneath your flag.

If war, for the Pentagon, became truly war against poverty, what you today spend on the cold or hot war would more than suffice to liquidate poverty here, and even to assure effective support to the war against poverty throughout the world.

Those out of work in the industries of the old war would find work in the industries mobilised by the new war to put an end to poverty.

Certainly you would at all costs have to give the example of complete respect for the first law of development: development is not achieved from outside. If the underdeveloped mass does not become aware and transform itself into the agent of its own development, there will only be a semblance of development, an illusion of development, but not real development in the true sense of the word.

Surely the arms race and the cold war have been tried already?

Set the world an example by giving a new and revolutionary aim to your military academies: make them a force against poverty, a force at the service of development and peace.

You could already give some signs of this change, which is far from being absurd and senseless:

—end the Paris talks, and make an immediate peace in Vietnam;

—take the initiative of bringing back Cuba into the American community and red China into the human community;

—radically revise the Alliance for Progress. Even change its name, for it has fallen into discredit. Call it—why not?—Alliance for Justice and Peace.

If you make use of the resources until now employed in the hot and cold wars—even if you give, as is natural, priority to the war against poverty within your own frontiers—and if these resources were used without any other aims and with a minimum of bureaucracy, you would begin to be regarded without contempt and without fear; with attention and sympathy, which is already the beginning of love:

—go to the heart of the problem of the gulf which grows daily wider between the developed world and the underdeveloped world, and insist on a fundamental revision of international trade policies.

Fraternal suggestions to Latin Americans

As for Latin America, it is obvious that our staff colleges would have even more to gain by reviewing the concept of war and adopting as a priority the war against underdevelopment and poverty.

And it is here, my North American friends, that you can and you must render us an immense service: when, in our hemisphere, such a proposal is interpreted as a desire to let the USSR have a free hand to make the world communist, help us to show how the concepts of capitalism and socialism have evolved, and how ingenuous it is to interpret the clash between economic empires as being, primarily, an ideological clash.

Nothing will so successfully remove from the underdeveloped countries the threat of polarisation and violence, nothing will prepare them better to live an authentic democracy, than a real chance of freeing themselves from poverty.

In a first stage if you do not achieve a fundamental revision of the terms of international trade, do not be surprised if we push Latin America to set up its own common market, in an effort to break out of your orbit—not, of course, to try to get into the Soviet one. It is simply criminal that we, Latin Americans, continue to sell our raw materials at more and more miserable prices, in order to buy them back, in manufactured form, months later, at prices which become more and more astronomical.

The sincerity of our aims will be demonstrated by a vigilance in avoiding internal imperialism, the sort of domination which could be practised by the bigger countries, such as Brazil.

If we set an example here, we have the hope of getting the Latin American armies:

—to declare total war on underdevelopment in our hemisphere;

—not to lend themselves to any attempt to protect privileged minorities when they label as subversive and communist peaceful movements to change socio-economic and politico-cultural structures which are responsible for internal colonialism, minorities whose wealth is based on the poverty of millions of their fellow-countrymen.

Just as our armies refused to pursue the slaves who fled to freedom, today they will refuse to assist in maintaining national slaves in the form of rural workers.

21

At the moment in my country, the executive power in the hands of the military has felt obliged to take over all the powers of government and to suspend practically all human rights; nor is this an isolated case in Latin America. If this temporary sacrifice of our liberties, if this risk of so many powers concentrated in human hands, resulted in necessary and inevitable basic reforms, great good would come out of evil.

But let those who want basic reforms not forget that they will be impossible if the people do not participate as agents of this change, and this implies serious work which until now certain groups in the army, in society at large and even groups in the church—perhaps well intentioned but poisoned by a narrow and one-sided anticommunism—have interpreted as subversion and communism.

I mean the awakening of the masses, human development, community organisation.

I know that I am suggesting both to North Americans and to Latin Americans tasks more complex and more difficult than opening a new canal between our hemispheres. And I am aware of all the other work which I have not mentioned, which needs to be done in the rest of the developed and underdeveloped world.

What is to be done?
CICOP believes in the effectiveness of moral forces: if it did not, there would have been no point in calling this conference.

The problem now is to go a little farther, to be a little more daring. Begin with the North American part: try to obtain from the universities evidence to prove the absurdity of world wars and local wars; try to obtain facts which show how all men can reach a human standard of living, thus putting an end to the scandal of the sub-men stuck in a sub-human life, trapped by sub-human work.

This is the starting point, the basic document for a dialogue with the Pentagon and for awakening the average man in the USA.

Am I wrong in thinking that the publicity organs of your country—though quite often controlled by economic power in its own interests—are powerful enough for people to use newspapers, radio and television to form an opinion and work out positions? Isn't there a chance here to awaken your people?

While you are acting on your side, we Latin Americans, in spite of all the risks, will try to complete our task.

God does not require his poor creatures to be successful, they are so strong in dreams, so weak in real possibilities of action. God requires us to devote ourselves to the service of our neighbour, to overcome our egoism, give ourselves entirely, without counting the cost.

When this happens, we shall have the right to hope that the Spirit of God will renew the face of the earth. What, ultimately, do we want? What are we struggling for?

We want to sweep poverty from the face of the earth, poverty which is an insult to the Creator. We want all human beings to be able to realise themselves in such a way that no one is reduced to being an object, a thing: we want all men to feel in themselves the image and likeness of the Father, to be in a position to fulfil their profound vocation as co-creators, charged by God with dominating nature and completing creation; we want human rights to be a reality.

Christ came on earth in order that men might have life, and have it in abundance. He goes further than our purely earthly desires; he gives us divine life.

Let us do our part with loyalty, sacrifice, and joy, and in the absolute certainty that God will do his.

3
A law for justice

Speech to the 6th World Congress of Catholic Jurists, Dakar (Senegal), December 1968.

If all men, and especially all christians, have duties towards law and justice, what can be said then of you, who are christian jurists? As jurists, all your life must be consecrated to proclaiming the law and fighting for justice. As christian jurists, the responsibility you bear on your shoulders is even more terrible.

Allow me to appeal to the jurists of the developed countries and the underdeveloped countries, separately and together. These are far from empty phrases: they are born of the hard-won experiences of millions of children of God, too often reduced to a sub-human condition. I feel keenly that I am lending a voice to those who suffer without having the possibility of proclaiming their own suffering; they feel exploited, without the power to denounce the exploiters, and reach the state of near-fatalism which thinks it is its destiny to submit to suffering on earth as the price, perhaps, of an eternal reward.

A fraternal message

To the jurists of the developed countries

Whatever your personal task in ordinary life, you must be aware of the extremely grave warning of the encyclical *Populorum Progressio*: in our day, it is inadequate to think of injustice as existing only between individuals and groups; today there is injustice between nations and even between worlds.

When one compares the aid received by the underdeveloped countries with the losses they suffer as a result of the deterioration in the prices of their raw materials in trade with the developed countries, and when one compares the developed countries' investments in the underdeveloped countries with the money which returns to the developed countries, it is easy to see that injustice in our time has taken on planetary proportions.

Would you not agree that in addition to your usual obligations you have another, of incomparable importance and exceptional urgency: that of denouncing the injustice in the relations between developed world and underdeveloped world? Since justice is the indispensable foundation of peace, international injustices place peace in the world in constant and growing danger.

Allow me furthermore to draw your attention to a very understandable temptation among those versed in the science of law: do not be content to denounce, with firmness and calm, the injustices between the two worlds. The time has come in which the jurist, without fear of losing a judge's calm, must give an example by committing himself entirely to the defence of justice, until it is fully respected.

You must be on the alert to denounce the trickeries which escape people of good faith who are not familiar with the malice of profiteers. For example, when you prove that the problem of the relations between the developed and underdeveloped countries is not one of aid at all but one of justice, there will be no lack of people to suggest paying higher prices for the raw materials of the underdeveloped countries, but the increased cost will be met, not by a decrease in their excessive profits, but from the public purse, making the 'reform' immoral and criminal.

Am I asking jurists to abandon their own field and invade the territory of the exchequer? I dream of jurists who do not move among abstractions, who are not up in the clouds, but who have their feet firmly on the ground that all men walk on, humble, glorious and slippery. . . .

Demand justice in the relations with the under-developed countries, but make it clear that the justice required must not be at the expense of the weak, but must mean a decrease in the excessive profits of the all-powerful.

Would it be too audacious to ask if all you jurists are aware of the effect on humanity of the international companies? International companies have no native land, no feelings. They are the real lords of the world, makers of so many wars and coups d'état.

The battle which must at all costs be fought against them would gain immense moral force if it could count on the support of those who defend the law, the men whose life is devoted to justice. The companies render impossible authentic development, in the sense of development of the entire man and of all men. Where they are set up—and they are set up all over the world —they stimulate economic growth for an extremely limited number of nations which ally themselves to them to exploit their own fellow-countrymen. There is no lack of people in any country who, like King Herod, ally themselves with the invaders: these are the herodians.

Why do not you jurists who work in international organisations take the initiative and give a world dimension to the antitrust law which the USA has drafted at national level? Is this beyond your powers? If you had seen what my eyes have seen, if you were to witness what is happening every day around me, you would understand my vehemence. What would Amos, Isaiah, Jeremiah, say today if they were living in Africa, Asia or Latin America? What would Christ say if he himself were talking to you this morning?

You must be aware that, twenty years after the solemn declaration of human rights by the UN, almost all these rights continue to be trampled on in the underdeveloped countries. Do you know that, very often, the foreign policy and trade of the developed countries is directly or indirectly responsible for the disregard of human rights in the Third World?

To the jurists of the underdeveloped countries
Jurists of the underdeveloped countries, you have tasks of your own.

Have you already felt the need for us to tackle the sins of the underdeveloped countries before we have the right to make demands on the developed world? Europe and the United States know that there are rich people in the underdeveloped countries who, instead of putting their money in development projects, keep their dollars in numbered accounts in Swiss and North American banks. Could you not discover an effective and democratic way of repatriating this money in such a way as to make it serve our effort of development?

We all know that one of the main obstacles to a more far-sighted policy towards the underdeveloped world is the reputation for dishonesty which weighs on the underdeveloped countries. Are our peoples really dishonest? No, not our peoples. But there are among us profiteers who become rich through fraud and bring a slur on the whole population. Would it be out of place, would it be without glory to ask you to find means to expose these disloyal citizens who, with their incorrect and unworthy attitude, compromise the good name of their country?

The other sin which, while not being the monopoly of our underdeveloped world, is certainly widespread in our regions, is to let laws fall into disrepute through not being enforced. Let me mention two of the most serious cases: it can hardly be news to you that there are many clever ways of getting round the law about sending profits abroad, nor will it surprise you to hear that very often in our countries, the government manages to promulgate laws for structural reform and creates the organs to apply them, and that in the end it all just remains on paper.

I beg you, do not say that the enforcement of laws is the business of the executive and their non-observance a matter for the police. Can you be unaware of the devaluation of laws? And what depreciates laws more than existing and not being enforced?

In the case of structural reforms, the young end up

with the impression that it is all a farce, no one is serious and, at least in Latin America, they then turn to radical action and violence.

Young people are irritated, above all, when they realise the hypocrisy of those who are interested in maintaining internal colonialism and defend their own privileges with slogans such as the struggle against communism, disorder and anarchy. Concentrate your moral force on unmasking these farces.

And when the situation is worsened by the presence of military groups who, consciously or unconsciously, are in the service of the privileged minorities, oppose force with law, skilfully but firmly, and take upon yourselves the responsibility for exposing the disorder, injustice and lack of humanity in the pseudo-order they see themselves committed to defending; denounce the abuses and ignominies committed by the two great imperialist blocs; the use of banners such as anti-communism, antisemitism and all the other antis, as a pretext for preserving inhuman structures and disreputable interests.

To the jurists of both worlds

Jurists of the developed and of the underdeveloped world, the problems I have raised are not new to you; in one way or another they must be on your minds already. And I know that with your education, your experience and your acuteness, you have already realised that any solution to them must involve a rethinking of structures, not only in the underdeveloped countries but also—however incredible this might seem—in the developed countries, with a view to the perfecting of relations between men.

Imagine a country which has 3,800,000 estates, with a total of 990 million acres, and finds almost half this area, 445 million acres, in the hands of 1% of the landowners. . . . Imagine too that of the above 3,800,000 estates, over two and a half million are small, economically unprofitable estates, tempting prizes for the great landowners. . . .

Tell me: does such a country, which is typical of the Latin American situation, or does it not demand a change in agrarian structure?

Imagine a country whose government is in process of increasing the number of primary school pupils and which is striving to answer to the needs of secondary and higher education, but which finds 88% of children leaving primary school before the fourth year, though in theory primary education is compulsory. . . . Suppose that in this country the situation gets worse as one goes higher up the system, until it reaches the scandalous point where higher education is limited to barely 1% of those who in theory have a right to it. Does such a country—the situation is typical of Latin America—need a complete overhaul of its socio-economic, political and cultural structures? You will know very well, faced with phenomena such as those I have just pointed out, that one could easily multiply examples in other fields, all going to show that it is not enough to change men and that there is no point in timid superficial reforms.

The underdeveloped countries cannot overturn their own iniquitous and outdated structures without alarming the developed countries which hold them in their sphere of influence, I would not say as colonies but, without doubt, as satellites. . . . There will immediately be talk of a threat to law and order (as though the crying injustice which keeps two-thirds of the population in a sub-human situation can be called order), of the danger of subversion and of communism.

The truth is that a change of structures in the under-developed world necessarily presupposes a change of structures in the developed world. If not, how, for example, shall we manage to achieve a change in the structure of industry or how shall we obtain justice in the international balance of trade?

Jurists would be rendering a remarkable service to humanity if they succeeded in making clear the truth of this assertion and managed to work out new structures for the developed and underdeveloped worlds.

If jurists of the developed world are surprised to find the developed countries included among those in need of alterations in structure, they should remember the important lesson of the encyclical *Populorum Progressio*: that for the development of the whole man and of all men, as important as the effort for the integral development of man is the union of all to achieve the harmonious development of humanity.

Would it be fantasy to imagine a new juridical organisation—closely synchronised with a new educative and religious organisation—capable of keeping up with the speed of change in other sectors of society?

A new maturity is demanded, and will be demanded more and more, in human history, agile enough to meet unforeseen situations and to reach rapid solutions to perfect international solidarity.

How can the means of mass communication be transformed into instruments to form free and critical opinion instead of being used in the service of group interests and ideological propaganda? How can an active personal participation be obtained in face of the problems created by bureaucracy and by the impersonal technology of power, where there is no longer personal responsibility and where the decisions are diffuse and neutral? How can we form human creatures capable of confronting the utilitarian mentality which scorns the *sense* of things and only values what is productive?

How can the law be led to an attitude of understanding and respect for civil disobedience, and even for the civil encroachment of pacifists?

If I am not mistaken, the answer will not be found in Kant and the neo-Kantians, nor in Hegel and the neo-Hegelians. Who knows whether the time has not come for the great affirmation of juridical personalism?...

Under obligation to Africa and Asia

Every time during a trip to Europe that I touch African soil, my Brazilian heart is seized by a profound emotion: my country, like others of Latin America, is under heavy obligations to Africa. Although christians, we Brazilians for three centuries committed the crime of maintaining Africans in degrading slavery. This lamentable episode reminds us all as christians, that we who are white and christian scandalised and continue to scandalise our non-christian brothers of Africa and Asia by our display of divisions between us and of covetousness and terrible injustice towards them.

Christian jurists, try to wipe out the memory of the sad examples of yesterday and today by openly supporting the underdeveloped world, faced with the injustices from which it suffers. Take up a position in such a clear and decisive way that it can even place at risk your jobs and, if need be, your very lives.

What a sad idea our Asian and African brothers have of whites and christians!... Try to create in their eyes a very different image, instead, not a caricature of Christ, but an image which arouses the desire to know intimately the friend of all men who, being Son of God, was made man and died on the cross to save not only the whites and the Europeans, but men of all races, of all colours, of all languages, of all cultures....

4
Impatience for change

April 1967

Is the encyclical *Populorum Progressio* on the same level as *Mater et Magistra* and *Pacem in Terris* or does it not correspond to what was expected of the Holy See on this subject?

Until the experts give their opinion, I would offer, as Archbishop of Recife, capital of the underdeveloped Brazilian north-east, the ten principal reasons why the encyclical will be decisive in our struggle for development.

1. *The gravest social problem of our time*

Those who exploit anticommunism as defence of their personal interests did not like hearing John XXIII in *Pacem in Terris* describe as the gravest social problem of our time the distance, daily growing greater, between the developed world and the underdeveloped world.

Paul VI's statement that 'the principal fact that we must all recognise is that the social question has become world-wide',[1] quotes specifically the celebrated declaration of his predecessor and recalls the confirmation brought to him by the *Pastoral Constitution on the Church in the Modern World*.

Whoever has to face almost invincible prejudices knows the value of these attitudes of John XXIII and Paul VI.

2. *Justice and peace*

The Pope says that the creation of the pontifical commission for justice and peace responds to a wish of the council and it is the contribution of the Holy See towards the great cause of the developing countries.

Paul VI affirms: 'Justice and peace is its name and its programme.' It is impossible to speak more clearly. The Holy See has taken up a position: it says that in the relations between the developed world and the underdeveloped world the problem is not simply one of aid, but one of justice; it is certainly aware that justice is lacking on a world scale; it recalls that without justice we shall never have peace.

Here we arrive at the heart of the problem of development and it is a joy to discover that the church has seen correctly. It is even more remarkable to see that the Holy Father has placed at the head of this key commission men—notably the chairman, Cardinal Rey, and the Secretary General, Gremmillion—who will certainly not allow it to become a sham for the third world, which greeted its creation with such joy.

3. *For an integral development of man*

Populorum Progressio sets out a whole programme

[1] Encyclical letter *Populorum Progressio*, translated as *The Great Social Problem*, London, Catholic Truth Society, 1967, para. 3.

with its definition of the integral development of man:

> Freedom from misery, the greater assurance of find-
> ing subsistence, health and fixed employment; an
> increased share of responsibility without oppression
> of any kind and in security from situations that do
> violence to their dignity as men; better education
> [para. 6],

a programme well summed up as: 'to seek to do more,
know more and have more in order to be more'.

4. *Theology of development*

Instead of a religion which promotes a fatalistic outlook on the world, the encyclical, following Vatican II,
presents man as having the right and the duty to
dominate nature and complete creation.

This is of enormous importance in the underdeveloped world, where sub-human conditions tempt
people to ascribe to God not only natural phenomena
(drought, floods), but also human injustices ('It is the
will of God: some are born poor, some are born rich').

With these directives, it is easy to present a religion
which is not in any way an opium for the masses; a
christianity which, instead of being alienated and
alienating, is incarnate as Christ.

5. *Property: a right which needs careful study*

Populorum Progressio sums up its teaching on property
with a quotation from the First Epistle of John:

> 'But if any one has the world's goods and sees his
> brother in need, yet closes his heart against him,
> how does God's love abide in him?' It is well known

how strong were the words used by the Fathers of the Church to describe the proper attitude of persons who possess anything towards persons in need. To quote Saint Ambrose: 'You are not making a gift of your possessions to the poor person. You are handing over to him what is his. For what has been given in common for the use of all, you have arrogated to yourself. The world is given to all, and not only to the rich.' That is, private property does not constitute for anyone an absolute and unconditioned right. No one is justified in keeping for his exclusive use what he does not need, when others lack necessities. In a word, according to the traditional doctrine as found in the Fathers of the Church and the great theologians, the right to property must never be exercised to the detriment of the common good. If there should arise a conflict between acquired private rights and primary community exigencies, it is the responsibility of public authorities to look for a solution, with the active participation of individuals and social groups. [para. 23]

6. *The use of income*

The council and the encyclical teach that 'the available revenue is not to be used in accordance with mere whim and that no place must be given to selfish speculation'. And both draw attention to those who, solely for their own advantage, send abroad considerable amounts of profit, the product of national resources and activity, without thinking of the 'manifest wrong' thus caused to their own country.[2]

[2] *Populorum Progressio*, 24.

7. *Liberal capitalism*

It is difficult to present a more realistic and more faithful synthesis of liberal capitalism than that presented by Paul VI:

> A system ... which considers profit as the key motive for economic progress, competition as the supreme law of economics, and private ownership of the means of production as an absolute right that has no limits and carries no corresponding social obligation. [*Populorum Progressio,* 26]

Recalling a statement of Pius XI, the encyclical denounces this unbridled liberalism as generator of 'the international imperialism of money'.

It is the very essence of anticommunist hysteria to cling to capitalism without even suspecting that it too is marked by inherent sins leading to deviations tragic for humanity.

8. *Extensions of the encyclical* Rerum Novarum

In an attempt to avoid economic dictatorship, Paul VI recommends that the principles of the encyclical *Rerum Novarum* be extended to cover relations between different countries.

A new name must be found for justice on a world scale. Obviously it will be stronger still if it is no longer concerned with relations between individuals, or between groups, but between peoples. . . .

9. *Revolution*

The whole world has already had its say: if it is true that the encyclical expresses serious reservations about violence, it nevertheless does admit it in exceptional cases.

The important thing, however, is to see and to feel, through the message of the Pope, that the church recognises that time is pressing and that it is madness to put off constantly changes of which the whole world stands in need.

10. *Civilisation in solidarity*

'If the grain of wheat does not die. . . .'

The church has adopted the favourite theses of the great Père Lebret, which can also be seen in some documents of the United Nations.

May the creator of IRFED, the originator of the idea of harmonious civilisation, the promoter of development, intercede for us with God.

Theoretically it seems easy for men to begin to live in harmony. In practice, it almost requires a miracle to avoid catastrophe.

Part 2

The dialogue of the century

Visiting Card

Among the greatest blessings of the council I must include meeting the bishops of the whole world in Rome and our surprise in noting that ideas, timidly but hopefully cherished, were shared by the five continents.

Several times, in the Basilica of St Peter's, I felt the temptation to intervene, to put forward figures, to make suggestions. I preferred to listen.

Here I am today, thinking aloud before brothers: presenting my ideas, raising questions, speaking as much to the bishops of one continent or even of one country, as to the bishops of the whole world. . . .

I thirst for dialogue: for the love of God, listen to me. . . .

5
Dialogue with the institutional church

Adapted from lectures during the Second Vatican Council.

The dialogue of the century

Let us recall the facts which cannot be forgotten and cannot become commonplaces repeated in a routine way without emotion or meaning:

—two thirds of humanity are in a state of under-development and hunger;

—between now and the year 2000 the situation will get worse—the earth's population will be over 6000 million, of whom 5000 million will be in the underdeveloped world;

—the saddest fact is that the fortunate and prosperous third is formed of christians, or of men under christian influence; the two-thirds living in hunger are, in an absolute majority, non-christian.

Pope John XXIII, in the encyclical *Mater et Magistra*, declared that this is perhaps the gravest social problem of our time. In practice, have we Catholics—and in particular we bishops—given this fact the importance it deserves and have we realised what we must do to put an end to this scandal?

It is easy to claim that this problem is so vast and of such a character as to be beyond our scope. It is easy to say that it is a socio-economic question which lies within the field of the state.

May I be allowed to recall that there is in this case a right and a duty for the church to intervene? First of all because everything is involved in the construction of the kingdom (all creation has until now been groaning in travail...hoping for redemption).

How can one remain indifferent to a collective injustice which affects two-thirds of humanity? How can one not be grieved by the knowledge that millions of human creatures are in a sub-human condition, without the possibility of using the divine gifts of intelligence and freedom? How can we not feel hard pressed before such a vast multitude, about which Christ will say to us, on the last day, 'I was hungry, I was thirsty, I was naked...'?

All of us bishops of the five continents could well, in a co-ordinated way and in the same spirit, try to promote dialogue between the developed world and the underdeveloped world.

All, in perfect synchronisation, should try to arouse the rich, not to give alms, but to practise social justice, by means of pastoral letters or collective declarations, sermons or conferences, specialised groups of independent background, in an effort to create a climate favourable to less egoism and more humane and christian feeling. If, at the end of a campaign con-

...ted with intelligence and devotion, we fail, we
...l at least have an easy conscience in the knowledge
...at we have tried our utmost.

Remember that:

—even in the underdeveloped regions, there is a
minority of rich people to be alerted. Of the rich of
Latin America, the *Economist* has said that 'not only
do they retain in their hands 80% of the land of the
continent, but often they control the parliaments and
possess a degree of idealism and faith in the future in
proportion to their deposits in the banks of Europe
and the United States (over 15,000 million dollars)';

—we must be aware that the work does not consist in
organising alms. Our aim is to make it understood that
the raising up of the underdeveloped world is a more
urgent and more serious problem than the East–West
conflict itself. Moreover, the church, by participating
in this movement, will inflict on communism a most
severe blow. We shall have to employ all our moral
forces to make understood the need to aid the underdeveloped two-thirds to stand on their own feet. Only
christianity will have enough authority to lead the
rich and powerful countries to understand the revolting paradox of not being loved precisely by the countries they are aiding most. It is difficult to *give*. The
right to give must be won by love. It is necessary to
overcome egoism to accept the fact that those one is
helping today are one's equals, competitors or con-
querors of tomorrow;

—the wish to see the church participate spiritually in
the struggle which will put an end to world injustice
does not mean leading the church out of its specific

46

field into an area which is not its own—which leads us to think of a christian Bandung. Imagine the moral repercussions in the whole world of an encounter—let us say in Jerusalem, half way between East and West—under the personal chairmanship of the Pope, of the bishops and christian technicians of Latin America, Asia and Africa. It would be less a matter of attaining concrete formulas and immediate solutions than of taking up a position, imparting a spirit, testing interest.

Stimulated by the Pontifical Commission for Latin America (CAL), a movement of spiritual and material aid for Latin America is in process of being set up in many countries of the developed world. In a dozen countries at least the hierarchies have constituted commissions for Latin America, concerned with sending priests, nuns and laity, with the distribution of financial aid or study grants.

It would be ungrateful not to recognise not only the purity of intention but also the real aid coming to us through the intervention of CAL. But let us point out that there is no system to this aid and also an absence of co-ordination between the various countries which provide it.

In the first phase of Vatican II, thanks to His Eminence Cardinal Leo-Joseph Suenens, an informal meeting was promoted between the bishops of the developed world and the bishops of the underdeveloped world. Once again a Cardinal of Malines took the initiative of a dialogue which, tomorrow, may lead to tangible consequences, like the conversations between Mercier and Lord Halifax.

On behalf of FERES, Father Houtart presented a

study on 'The Church of Latin America at the time of the Council' (a synthesis based on the twenty sociological studies, on the five documents and on the sixteen socio-religious studies which FERES[1] had already published on the Latin American continent). Two obvious immediate needs emerged:

—the need to tackle the key points discovered by the studies carried out (instead of the terrible squandering of apostolic activities which may be full of supernatural and often heroic purpose but do not tackle the most serious, most urgent and explosive problems, and where there is little preparation for the future or for continuity of action). Revolutionary movements arise in general through embodying profound aspirations and real appeals to justice. In the present case, where the danger of a Marxist revolution is clear, the most important thing is not to fight *afterwards*, it is to provide a farsighted action which can answer these aspirations;

—the need to co-ordinate the different commissions for Latin America among themselves and with CELAM.

At the time of the meeting sponsored by Cardinal Suenens, FERES gave us a vision of the *whole* underdeveloped world, without being limited to Latin America, along the lines of the study of Father Houtart, L. Grond and C. Thoen: 'The Church and aid to the developing countries'.

Several other initiatives reveal, on the part of the hierarchy of the two worlds, an intelligent and pro-

[1] International Federation of Catholic Institutes for Social and Socio-Religious Studies.

foundly evangelical concern. Here are some typical examples:

—Pax Christi has posed in a precise way the problem of the duties of christians with regard to development;

—in Chile, the episcopate—acting fully within its specific mission—published a collective pastoral plan which anticipated the grave and clearsighted opinion presented by the special number of *Mensaje* on 'Revolution in Latin America: the Christian outlook';

—in Brazil, the episcopate, after stimulating the government to launch a plan of socio-economic recovery for the North-East (the most critically underdeveloped region of the country), is undertaking, along the lines of the Colombian experiment, a vast and intelligent movement of basic education by means of radio schools.

We have no lack of meaningful partial movements. Neither do we lack the beginnings of a collective conscience. But much remains for us to do in order for us not to give a false impression of connivance in an unjust and outdated social order.

A new catechesis

There are among us many who should perhaps review, study in depth and develop the idea of catechesis.

As a general rule catechesis means the teaching of religion in a formal way by catechists who use a religious textbook. In this approach the problems are improving the manual, training the catechists and trying to reach not only the children but also adolescents and adults. Since the (western) Code of Canon Law now demands that the Congregation of Christian

Doctrine should function in every parish, there have been sincere efforts to implement section 2 of canon 711.

What would become of the church and humanity if there only existed catechesis in the formal sense? Most of the underdeveloped two-thirds of humanity would live beyond its scope; the workers too, for Pius XI emphasised this and the facts continue to prove him right: the church has lost the working class and the absolute majority of adults in the big cities, for as a general rule among them the percentage of attendance at Sunday mass (practically the only formal chance remaining to the church) does not exceed 10%.

More important than insisting on the negative factors, positive factors or constructive suggestions must be put forward.

We may claim a victory in Latin America for the experiment—begun in Colombia and transplanted to several other countries—of basic education through radio schools.

We are not dealing here with a simple formal catechesis, because the organisers had the sense to see that there was, right from the outset, a preliminary task, human and christian, to be performed: that of setting on their feet thousands of human creatures who were in a sub-human condition: that of helping them to win the preliminaries of freedom (what is the use of talking about freedom and human rights to those who have no home, no real nourishment, no proper clothing, nor the minimum of education, of leisure or religious aid, nor even a minimum guarantee of work?)...

By means not only of a radio programme but of a

radio school (made possible thanks to the transistor, even in extremely backward areas where there is no electricity), the spirit of initiative is awakened, the sense of collaboration, the courage to live, the thirst for progress.

In Brazil, the experiment is advancing in quantity and improving in quality. For example, in the formation of the team responsible for each Catholic transmission and for the formation of the indispensable monitors (the soul of the radio school), we took over and adapted to the Brazilian situation methods employed in France by popular educators.

The christians of the developing world give themselves to the work of basic education, fully respecting and collaborating with the non-Christians. They are fulfilling an important duty of human solidarity. They know, it is true, that the education transmitted will also be able to serve as basis for future catechesis.

This leads us to think:

—of the advantage of an exchange of experiences in basic education between Latin America, Africa and Asia;

—of the enrichment that human and christian formation (catechesis) could receive if organs such as the International Institute of Catechesis and Pastoral Care, or the International Centre of Studies of Religious Formation at Brussels, were to unite for a study in common with specialists in basic education from several regions of the underdeveloped world.

Since we have mentioned the famous International Institute of Catechesis and Pastoral Care in Belgium— the homeland of Cardijn, the founder of the Young

Christian Workers—this leads us to think of the broadening of catechesis which would result from the official recognition *as catechesis* of any effort at formation carried out in the home or work situation by militants, not only of the YCW but of any specialised Catholic organisation.

Official catechesis would gain by this, as would also the militants, for the specialists in catechesis could enrich still more the famous method of 'seeing, judging and acting' which, only quite recently in the encyclical *Mater et Magistra,* received its consecration on the part of the Holy See. If no such action is taken, how can the working class masses be reached who continue to elude us in such a distressing way?

As for the immense masses of the big cities who do not even have a minimum of weekly contact with the Church through Sunday mass, we should regard *as catechesis* the efforts (which can always be improved) not only of specialised Catholic organisations but of institutions such as the Christian Family Movement or the Legion of Mary.

What is to be done with the intellectuals, who are also eluding us so dangerously? What in particular is to be done for the scholars and artists? Who has already experience in this field?

There is a word to be said on the young in the countries where the mass of the population is educated mainly while they are young and where the number of those who can begin studies and follow them through is low. Sometimes the young students are more aware of the great national and international problems than the professors themselves. It would be anti-psychological and unjust to say simply that they are ignorant.

This would be committing the grave mistake of getting annoyed because they are concerned with subjects which are more alive and important and explosive than the customary routine subjects imposed on them. What intelligent and open catechesis could be undertaken in the centres of higher learning?

Sometimes—it must be recognised, although taking care to avoid excesses and abuses—especially in environments such as those of islam or marxism, the only possibility we have is a catechesis of fraternal presence and the friendly example of an unpretentious life. Is not the life of the little brothers and sisters of Père de Foucauld a catechesis?

We and our clergy

Preliminary remarks:

—when we speak of our clergy, we are thinking just as much of the secular clergy (an expression which we should change), as of the regular clergy, residing in our diocese (especially if it is totally or in part devoted to the external apostolate); not only of the national clergy but also of the foreign clergy;

—we base ourselves on the principle that any bishop (at least theoretically) is convinced that he can do nothing without his clergy.

Let us put an end, once and for all, to the image of the prince-bishop living in a palace, isolated from his clergy, whom he keeps coldly at a distance. Let us put an end to everything which can give the priests the impression that they are not seen and known except through the grille of the diocesan curia, when paying contributions or dealing with demands. Let us put an end to the image of the authority which in reality sets much more store on making itself feared than on being loved, on being served than on serving.

Who does not know that in order for an episcopal decision to be hindered from being carried out in a parish, it is not even necessary for the parish priest to combat it: he only needs to remain reticent and aloof? To answer for the flock which God has entrusted to us, to participate in the total effort of the ecclesiastical province, of the region and of the country, to give life to the world, and more and more abundant life, one must, for a start, pay the necessary price (and we shall be pointing out others), i.e. join up as a team with the clergy and win their confidence, by loving them in actions and in truth, by being one with them.

There are some pastoral visitations which give the impression of being 'promotions' of the bishop (in the publicity sense of the word), of being an inspection of the parish priest and a heavy expense for the faithful. The ideal would be not to be just visitors but to act as though we were going home: to go there to encourage and to be an instrument of sanctification for the parish priest and for the faithful.

What we can desire for our clergy in relation to a work plan and to a total pastoral effort will only be obtained to the degree in which:

—we give an example of cooperation with the other bishops of the region, the country, the continent and the world;

—the priest sees in us the Good Shepherd, the Father, the imitator of him who did not come to be served but to serve.

It is a poor bishop who gives the impression of having remembered from the gospel only the scene of the expulsion of the moneychangers from the Temple, forgetting dozens of other scenes of pure and infinite mercy. Life teaches us that if goodness cannot solve everything, what goodness cannot solve cannot be solved by violence either. Violence engenders rebels, hypocrites or cowards according to the personality of those affected by it.

Let us give our clergy, among other things, the following examples:

—of planned work, with the aid of specialists of real competence;

—of a *permanent* effort of sanctification in the sense of living sanctifying grace and in the style of spirituality proper to someone who has been called by Providence to be in the world, though not of it.

—of a proper hierarchy of activities, giving to essentials the value of the essential and to the relative the value of the relative;

—of methodical study, linked to our profound vocation and to the duty of our state.

With whom, other than ourselves, will our priests and above all our parish priests learn:

—to celebrate the holy sacrifice (celebrations which are impossible to follow give scandal to the laity, especially where the use of missals is widespread);

—to administer the sacraments—and the effort to achieve a community liturgy which people can begin to understand and take part in must not turn into a source of scandal for the faithful;

—to proclaim the word of God; there is a grave crisis in preaching. Now, strictly speaking, the right and the duty to preach only belongs to the bishop. From us must come the example of a living and life-giving preaching;

—to spend time in training laymen whom we could confidently entrust with everything which is not specifically priestly (what a beautiful and effective way to increase our members!).

Let us give to the clergy (and to the laity) the example of not jumping at shadows; of rejoicing in having around us priests holier, more intelligent, more cultured, more hard-working, cleverer, better understood and better loved than ourselves. Let us try to promote the family spirit which will allow us to put in common all the joys and all the sorrows, hopes and cares, work and burdens of each.

Let us keep aloof from intrigues and let us be incapable of reading an anonymous letter (anyone who has not the moral courage to answer for his information and accusations does not merit the respect of being heard).

When a priest is sick—in body or soul—he deserves the care one would give to a son. When he is old, tired, beaten, he must find in us a father. When he is in danger, and especially when he falls, he must, more than ever, discover Jesus Christ in us.

How can one, especially in dioceses without resources and with a poor population, tackle the problem of supporting the clergy? How can we come to the aid of priests in cases of accident, old age or permanent illness?

Will we have the courage to think of those brothers in the priesthood who have fallen by the wayside?... There are those who wish to return (and at least on the occasion of a jubilee should be re-admitted to the celebration of holy mass, even if they have committed the folly of having attempted a civil contract of marriage). There are those who prefer to keep their family but who dream of the possibility of leading a sacramental life.

All these considerations and many others which can occur to each of us, lead us to think of the seminaries. To the degree in which we can fully answer for the houses of formation of our clergy, we shall be able to attempt—with the grace of God and the aid of specialists—to attain the exact degree of *aggiornamento*, which avoids the risks both of falling into routine and of being imprudent.

We shall also have to see that the education of our clergy keeps pace with new developments—and here again the example must come from us. Even in places where there is a heavy load of work, we may be able to find a way for bishops to do more up to date studies. The aim would not be to turn us into specialists but to give us a modern view of the world and make it easier for us to accept our position as the vanguard of the church in our diocese, a position inherent in our appointment as bishops.

If, from the civil point of view, we are foreigners, let us try to relive the experience of Saint Paul, to make ourselves all things to all men in order to win all for Jesus Christ. Let us try to identify ourselves to the full with the countries to which Providence has sent us, and with the people who have been set apart for us from all eternity. Let us not feel strangers, let us try to understand the aspirations of nationalism which are so violent today, but ultimately rooted in the plans of Providence. Hence the sacred duty—in union with the Holy Father—of fully adopting the role of forerunners, preparing for our withdrawal and the rise of the indigenous clergy.

If from the civil point of view, we are not foreigners, let us be understanding and kind to the foreign priests. Let us keep watch among the indigenous clergy, among the laity, among the authorities, to make less painful the sacrifice of those who have abandoned all to come to help us to evangelise our country (though obviously without neglecting the formation of a holy and effective local clergy).

If all that has been recalled here was valid in any circumstances whatever, it all seems to us more valid still in face of the absolute need to promote a 'post-council' at the same level as the council itself. How can we pass from beautiful written schemes to living reality without the full aid and the absolute collaboration of our clergy?

Practical conclusions on the laity

More important than arriving at exact definitions, our beautiful theory on the laity must be translated into everyday actions. And it happens that clericalism is instinctive in us, i.e. the practical neglect of the proper and irreplaceable function that God reserves for the laity, situated at a point of liaison between the church and the world.

There are those who maintain that they do not have available laymen of confidence and worth. Is it unjust to say that we have the laity we deserve? If someone does not spend time in forming his laity, how can he hope for good, educated laymen to fall out of the blue?

If our parish priests see us, on the diocesan plane, utilising the laity in the royal, priestly and prophetic function of the Church, they will know how to mobilise the laity in an adequate manner by calling them to collaborate in transforming more and more the parish and community of faith, of worship and of charity.

How can such a community of faith be achieved without the layman helping us to evaluate preaching, make teaching alive and forceful, promote and stimulate the biblical movement?

How can a community of worship be achieved without leading the faithful, not only in external attitudes, but to a more and more profound sense of worship?

How can a community of charity be achieved without making of each christian an apostle, a militant, who assumes the responsibility for evangelising and transforming with the spirit of the gospel all areas of life and all those living in them?

Why not admit, theoretically and in practice, the preparatory and complementary function which falls to laymen, notably in relation to temporal problems? In our world of the faith, spiritually divided and separated, why not give back its just worth to the role of the laity in the defence and the proclamation of the faith and in the regeneration of society?

We must constantly be on our guard against clericalism. The habit of speaking down from the pulpit

59

to a passive audience which has not the right to react, fixes us in the mental attitude of always speaking 'ex cathedra', like someone who is master in all fields, like someone who must have the last word on all subjects.

It is a duty of the hierarchy to stimulate the layman to open new horizons by assuring him of his full confidence (and not only by appealing to prudence, frequently necessary, but yet so negative). The daring men of today prepare the normal attitudes of tomorrow. The church is not an organisation which immobilises, but one which involves. Do the laymen who take up more daring positions feel confidence, encouragement, positive criticism, or distrust on the part of the bishops? Does one not see, normally, in the church an attitude of hypocrisy through which the hierarchy is only half informed and where its advice is heard with respect but without interest? Most often is not the cause the obvious lack of information of the bishops and their fear of innovations?

In general, we are not well prepared for the dialogue with the laity. We are more used to an association in which the members listen silently and respectfully agree with us, than to groups of militants who use their own heads and who have the courage and the confidence to say what they think. It also happens that it is not possible to count, in difficult moments, on vague and accommodating individuals.

Given the fact that we are always in a hurry, it is simpler and easier to act oneself than to stop to learn, although the task may be one which a layman would accomplish just as well, or much better, than we.

In thinking of the senate around the Pope, we can

and we must take care to maintain near it laymen who are the direct spokesmen of the laity and specialists in the various specific fields. It is very significant that the Holy See should be so insistent on calling the world congresses of the lay apostolate, and we would do well to meditate on the holiness, education and efficiency of the laity as shown in these meetings.

It has already been said that in apocalyptic eras we seek the collaboration of the laity and then in Constaninian periods we ignore them. Let us integrate the laity once for all—in theory and in practice—into the structure of the church. In difficult times as in easy times, where there is a shortage of clergy and where there is a surplus, let us recall that the layman has his own mission which it is not for us to exercise. We must not forget that normally it is not for us to take a position on specific solutions on the temporal plane. It is the specific domain of the layman; we must have confidence in him and respect his choices in this sector.

Let us examine our consciences and ask ourselves: have we transmitted to the faithful the *spirit* and the orientation of the council? Have we stopped at merely external actions, in the sumptuousness of the ritual, in the joy of meeting bishops from other countries, in speaking to an Asian or sitting next to an African?

The recovery of poverty

There is one thesis which can be historically proved: before undertaking profound reforms, the church has always come to terms again with poverty. In the light of this it seems providential that in Rome, during the first phase of Vatican II, the Poverty Group was set up,

61

bishops from all over the world who joined to study the mystery of the poor and to discover the practical means to aid the church to find again the lost paths of poverty.

Again, in the effort towards union with our separated brethren, even more important than an examination of points of doctrine is the return to poverty.

Here are some practical suggestions which may serve as point of departure for fraternal conversations of great importance.

Let us take the initiative in abolishing our personal titles of Eminence, Beatitude, Excellency. Let us reject the folly of considering ourselves nobles and let us renounce our coats of arms and our devices. These seem to be things of no importance, but how much all this separates us from our clergy and from our faithful! It separates us from our century which is already adopting a different way of life. It separates us above all from the workers and the poor.

Let us ourselves simplify our style of dress. Let us not allow our moral force and our authority to depend on the make of our car. Let us pay serious attention to our residences. It is right that in liturgical functions a certain splendour should be preserved (without however reaching excesses which, in some areas, could appear an affront). But in everyday life, attention to episcopal crosses and extremely valuable rings and (to give another example, in relation to the countries where the soutane is the dress of the clergy) attention to shoes with silver buckles, is ridiculous and improper today. There are small cars, the use of which is understood and accepted by everyone. There are cars which scandalise and revolt. Let us not allow our houses to be called palaces. But let us also make sure that they *really* are not palaces.

Even where the house of God is concerned, the moment has come to review the problem of its construction. Without doubt, we shall always make ours the words of Solomon on the consecration of the Temple of Jerusalem and we shall always keep present the word of Christ to Judas in defence of Magdalen. But in a world where two-thirds of the people are in a state of underdevelopment and hunger, how can we squander huge sums on the construction of temples of stone, forgetting the living Christ, who is present in the person of the poor? And when shall we come to understand that in too sumptuous churches the poor have not the courage to enter and do not feel at home?

Remembering that the church is not attached to styles and to types of construction; remembering that it has always been skilled at placing at the service of God the material and the techniques of every century; remembering above all the ever-growing poverty in our time of millions of men, contrasting in a revolting way with the comfort and the luxury of a small number; remembering too that, even if we add up all the christian families, we are a minority and a declining minority at that, let us stimulate young architects to invent types of churches:

—which are beautiful and simple, liturgical and functional;

—which arouse and nourish the religious sense without a shadow of ostentation and arrogance.

May the houses of God rise, more than ever, frater-

63

nally mixed with the houses of men: open, welcoming, *poor* in the evangelical sense.

Until now everything we have discussed, although important, is only to a certain degree external. The essential thing is the mentality.

Let us have the courage to carry out a revision of conscience and of life: have we, or have we not, adopted a capitalist mentality, with methods and procedures which would be all very well for bankers but which are perhaps not very proper for someone who is *another Christ*?

In our concern to provide endowments for the curia, for parishes or for institutions, are we still keeping within the limits acceptable to those who, in the eyes of men, incarnate the doctrine of the gospel?

Are there not cases of churches which are large landowners? Are there not cases of dioceses which are unjust towards their workers, their officials and their teachers?

We are speaking of mentality. An interesting examination to carry out is to see how far our language (and the word is, or should be, the incarnation of the thought) is bourgeois. We know how to talk to the rich and to the middle class; do we also know how to talk to the workers and to the poor?

Another very serious thing to meditate on—before God, who is not deceived—is the treatment we give to the rich. The ideal would be that, before the rich— without humiliating, without wounding, without a trace of hatred, without exaggerating, addressing ourselves preferably to limited audiences—we should not falsify or tone down too much the striking counsels that Jesus Christ left us. Let them not accuse us before our judge of having capitulated and become connivent and tame as a result of the alms we receive. The story is told that St Francis of Paola once received gold coins from the King of Naples, who had been carrying on some unjust dealings. The saint broke one of the coins miraculously, and blood ran out. Is there not sweat and blood in the alms we receive?

All this alteration in outlook demands a study in depth of the theology of poverty. It has been said with reason that our manuals of theology devote too much space to the treatise on purity and certainly speak less (and in a way which is not at all up to date and courageous) of the seventh commandment. It has been rightly said that the scene of the Last Judgment should be studied just as deeply, from the doctrinal point of view, as those passages of the Scriptures such as 'Thou art Peter' or 'This is my body.'

The post-conciliar period is just as important as the council

It would indeed be a pity if Vatican II managed to produce extremely fine decrees but that these decrees remained dead letters and were never applied. They would soon be covered in discredit and ridicule.

However we are not under any illusions: it is easier to hold a council than to put its decisions into practice. As always, here are some suggestions we could discuss. But let us be loyal to one another and to the church: it is not enough to know the conclusions and to listen to erudite talks on them. We must dwell on them, in a sincere desire to understand them and to adopt them.

Only someone convinced and enthusiastic will succeed in transmitting the flame. We shall have to fire our clergy and our laity with the spirit of the council, by exhorting them to be, with the aid of divine grace, the missionaries of Vatican II. More than ever, we shall need *holiness*, holiness on the part of our clergy, holiness on the part of our laity.

It is only to the degree in which we live the divine life in us and our unity in Christ that we shall be able to transform the conclusions of the council into a sacred mission to be accomplished, into a reform to be undertaken. The model to have always before our eyes will be, among others, for us bishops St Charles Borromeo.

We must *win over* our clergy to the conclusions of the council. This will be easy with conclusions they approve of. It will be difficult, but essential, in the case of conclusions which do not attract them or which run contrary to the manifest or hidden aspirations of our clergy. Without this collaboration we shall risk talking in vain.

Let us mobilise the laity to aid us in turning the conclusions of the council into real life and in translating them into action. The conclusions must reach families, professional circles, leisure activities, educational establishments, all sectors of life or activity. We must make intelligent use of the means of publicity and the techniques of diffusion of ideas and of group discussion.

Let us take particular care to lead the different christian families and the non-christian groups to an awareness of the council's conclusions. We must try everything that can foster good will, prepare the way, open doors, predispose to dialogue.

Probably the work of our theologians will have to be complemented:

—by sociologists to plan the adaptation of the general conclusions of the council to the different continents, regions or countries;

—by the representatives of the different areas of life or work so that the message of the council can reach all men in intelligible terms, while safeguarding doctrine.

If we have already taken care to ask for sacrifices and prayers on behalf of the council while it was in progress, we shall have to count even more on prayers and sacrifices for the council to transform itself into living reality.

The sick, the children and those souls specially consecrated to God will merit our particular attention. Let us have the humility to ask non-Catholic christians, and even non-christian believers, to pray with us for the implementation of the council. Let us mobilise the church suffering and the church triumphant towards the mission that Providence entrusts to us: taking Vatican II—with Peter at the head and under the action of the Holy Spirit—from theory to practice.

Let us mutually exchange information on the post-conciliar period in our dioceses, our countries, our continents. Let us transform the difficulties or the victories of each of us into victories or difficulties of the whole church.

6
Internal colonialism

Closing speech to CEPAL *course, Salvador de Bahia, Brazil, August 1966.*

Is it reasonable to have agreed, at a day's notice, to deliver the closing speech at a specialised course organised by BNDE (National Bank of Economic Development), by SUDENE (Superintendence for the Development of the North-East) and by CEPAL (Economic Commission for Latin America) under the auspices of the United Nations? It would certainly not be if my purpose were to present to the technicians yet one more lecture in their own subject.

But the reasons which have led me here fully justify my presence, which I wish to be, to some degree, the evocation of the presence at the United Nations of the pilgrim of peace. Paul VI has reminded technicians of the existence of 'experts in humanity'.

Whoever wishes to belong to a group of technicians of this sort:

—whether belonging to a race, a continent, a country,

68

a region, must try to think, to speak and to act above all as a human being bound fraternally to all humanity;

—although addressing himself to important groups, and doing as much as possible to reach the people who, to greater or lesser degree, enjoy the power and take the decisions, he must have the firmness of someone who has a message to transmit, but at the same time he must do so with the humility of someone who claims to serve and bear truth in charity, the more carefully, in view of the fact that the truth to be transmitted will be more demanding.

Technicians of economic development, who have had the goodness to invite me to deliver this speech, I am certain that you expect me to speak to you as a 'technician of humanity', as a disciple of the pilgrim of peace, as an apostle of Jesus Christ.

You will then allow me to go directly to certain points which seem to me to be of extreme gravity and which present a real challenge for us all.

Without fear of repeating myself, I should like to dwell on a suggestion I have already made on more than one occasion but which, until today, has fallen on deaf ears. I commit it through you to CEPAL, which is just as indispensable in the American continent as SUDENE is in Brazil.

An urgent campaign

If I am not mistaken, one of the most fitting initiatives, and one richest in consequences for the future of development, was the meeting at Geneva, from March to June 1964, of the United Nations conference on trade and development. One day, history will do justice to CEPAL: it was very clearsighted in calling this meeting. There, finally, the root of the problem was reached. The statement was calm and objective, based on figures: the relations between the developed world and the underdeveloped world are in a bad state. And this was said without violence or demagogy, without ingratitude or unilateral outlook. The other aspects of development were not forgotten, but it was demonstrated, and in an irrefutable way:

—that it is not enough to see that, as a whole, the developed world does not manage to contribute even 1% of its gross national product to the development of the whole of the underdeveloped world;

—that it is not sufficient to prove that wars and the arms race consume and will continue to consume sums several times greater than those devoted to development;

—that the problem is not one of trying to make development aid increase to 1% or 2%—for it is not a matter of aid, but rather of justice on a world scale.

The world was astonished when Paul Prebisch proved that, over the last ten years, Latin America has had to pay back to the developed world over 13,000 million dollars.

History will recall the equally lamentable egoisms of the USSR and of the USA, which both proved unable to face up to such a grave denunciation and tried to torpedo it. Nevertheless it is still more urgent to end this injustice—I repeat, an injustice on a world scale —than to destroy the stocks of atomic bombs.

History will remember that, two years after the famous meeting, it had not been possible to create, even within the United Nations, beside UNESCO and ILO, a real world trade organisation. Until now we have had to be content with a mere 'Council for trade and development'.

Credit should be given to the Second Vatican Ecumenical Council: in dealing at length with development—which John XXIII had already stated in the encyclical *Pacem in Terris* to be the most important social problem of our time—it recalled what had happened at Geneva and gave all its support to the thesis of CEPAL by affirming it in the *Pastoral Constitution on the Church in the Modern World* (86):

> The international community should see to the coordination and stimulation of economic growth. These objectives must be pursued in such a way, however, that the resources organised for this purpose can be shared as effectively and justly as possible. This same community should regulate economic relations throughout the world so that they can unfold in a way which is fair. In so doing, however, the community should honour the principle of subsidiarity.
>
> Let adequate organisations be established for fostering and harmonising international trade, especially with respect to the less advanced countries, and for repairing the deficiencies caused by an excessive disproportion in the power possessed by various nations. Such regulatory activity, combined with technical, cultural, and financial help, ought to afford the needed assistance to nations striving for progress, enabling them to achieve economic growth expeditiously.

At first sight, it may seem ridiculous and even absurd to imagine that an idea, even a correct and exact one, can dominate economic interests stronger than the strongest states. But history is full of examples of ideas which end up by causing the fall of interests which seemed all-powerful. It is enough to recall, at national level, the struggle for the abolition of slavery led by young people such as Castro Alvez, Rui Barbosa and Joaquim Nabuco. At an international level, we can think of the victories of the workers.

There are urgent reasons for Don Quixote to enter the lists once more. And only the ingenuous and those without creative imagination still think that Quixotism means idealism without practical consequences, for these are the ideas which lead the world.

It is an urgent necessity to launch a worldwide campaign for the abolition of slavery, i.e. to demand that the political independence of peoples should be completed by their economic independence—not only of certain social classes or of certain regions of the world, but of the whole man and of all men.

This is urgent because it is no exaggeration to say that the peace of the world is at stake. The young, the young in particular, are losing patience and falling into violence and desperate extremism. It must be demonstrated that democratic methods are worth something. It is essential to make an immense effort to save whole peoples from lamentable and inhuman internal struggles, and to liberate humanity from a world conflict whose consequences cannot be foreseen.

CEPAL could perhaps approach the United Nations and provoke a movement of public opinion which would mobilise, among other forces, the universities, the communications media, religious and intellectual leaders, employers' and workers' leaders, political leaders.

The universities

If the attention of the universities of the developed and underdeveloped world is drawn to the gravity of the declaration made in Geneva in 1964, by means of suitable instruments, such as, for example, of objective reports of indisputable technical value, they will get going. The problem is to convince them. We can count straight away on the enthusiastic sympathy among students for just and human causes. And no university in any part of the world will lack idealistic professors, openminded and enquiring, ready to examine the facts in all objectivity and give their support to the causes for which they will have been won over.

Let us repeat: the work to be undertaken will consist in examining whether it is necessary to reformulate the problem of the economic relations between the developed world and the underdeveloped world and whether it is possible to re-examine the system of 'aid', because we are concerned here with injustice on a world scale.

The project will involve special research by both the universities of the wealthy countries and those of the underdeveloped countries. In the underdeveloped world, it will for example be necessary to examine more profoundly what is meant by 'internal colonialism'. In the developed world, it will be useful to examine how poverty disfigures the human person.

The communications media

The communications media—newspapers, magazines, radio, TV—possess the antennae capable of closely following the movement which will break out in the universities.

Today, the big newspapers have specialised editors, of university standard, who are expert researchers. And the international services take it upon themselves to keep the less important newspapers well informed.

The press, in dealing with the underdeveloped world, has already got over the stage of exoticism and has contributed in a decisive way to making public opinion conscious of the poverty and hunger which are spreading more and more over the earth. The press must then be invited to give its collaboration to a movement of public opinion which has the aim of convincing the ordinary man in the rich countries that he must refuse to give his support to an injustice with such tragic consequences, and to show the ordinary man in the poor countries that egoism is not a monopoly of the rich countries.

Religious and intellectual leaders

In the time of John XXIII and of Paul VI, the happy ecumenical climate in which we live allows the organisation in many places all over the world—with rare and sad exceptions—of meetings of heads of different religions who are all preoccupied with peace, who all know that peace without justice is a utopian dream.

Quite obviously, we also wish to have with us the agnostics and even the atheists, on the sole condition that they hunger after truth and justice. How many of them I have known who are christian in their attitudes!

Employers and workers

There are among managers a good number of sensitive men who wish to be human and just. The evil is the system which crushes them and which they cannot manage to escape. They must be called, listened to, spoken to, they must be made to meet others, many others, who feel the same things and suffer the same constraint.

As for the workers, it is enough to remind them that the workers of the developed world, who are already under the threat of becoming bourgeois through having attained a relatively high standard of living, will recall that there are, around the world, many 'sub-workers'.

Political leaders

As you see, I am doing no more than point out the work to be done. If CEPAL considers worthy of examination the suggestion I give you to pass on to it, it will be very easy, with your help, to refine our proposal. If the United Nations decided to give its support to the movement of public opinion I have suggested to you here, we should obviously not leave it at these broad outlines.

In any case, I do not wish to forget that in the world of politics, just as much on the side of executive power as on that of legislative power, there are, in every country, men who are aware of and open to great causes, ready to fight, and accustomed to fighting.

My friends, in delivering this message to you, in passing on this appeal, I would not be being sincere to myself or to you if I did not add a last word which I ask you to keep and meditate on: if it is true that economic liberation is indispensable as complement of political liberation, it nevertheless does not account for all human necessities, for it does not in itself entail the total liberation of man. Study this sentence deeply: only the saints are totally free.

7
Capitalism against peace

Contribution to a world congress of Catholic youth movements, West Berlin, April 1968.

God gives me the joy of loving the young and of believing in them. For example, insofar as peace is made by men, I believe that it will be much more the work of the young than of adults.

The adult, in general, is less generous and more egoistic, more distrustful, colder. The outlook of the adult is very often tarnished with self-interest. This is why one of the strongest temptations which the young face is that of seeing idealism diminish, enthusiasms grow cold, the capacity for adaptation take over, as young people set themselves up in life and think—as is quite natural—of marrying, of getting a house, of having children and of seeing to their future.

Allow me to take advantage of this exceptional opportunity of talking to young people who represent millions of the young from North and South (i.e. from the developed countries and from the underdeveloped countries), to list the main obstacles blocking the roads to peace.

Obviously I have not the least intention of shattering your enthusiasm; at your age, the more difficult the objective, the more alluring it becomes. See what a magnificent temptation it is to apply oneself fully, and with all one's heart, head and faith, through innumerable obstacles, to constructing peace!

Obstacles on the road to peace

A fraternal message to the young people of the capitalist developed countries

Can capitalism cease to consider profit as the essential motor of economic progress, competition as the supreme law of the economy, and private ownership of the means of production as an absolute right, without limits, without corresponding social obligations? These principles, which seem inherent in the very essence of capitalism, lead to absurdities and to revolting injustices which compromise the development of the whole man and of all men (and we know that development is the new name for peace, as we also know that without justice no authentic development will ever exist, and consequently that peace will never exist).

Look at the main fruits—rotten fruits—of capitalist egoism:

—in Latin America (does this also happen in Africa and Asia?) internal colonialism is spreading. This means a small group of privileged people in Latin America itself whose wealth is maintained at the expense of the poverty of millions of their fellow-citizens. The owners of huge tracts of land keep most of it uncultivated. They allow poor families to live and

78

work there. But to prevent them from acquiring any rights, care is taken that they are kept in foul hovels and work under a patriarchal regime without any law to support them. This is unquestionably a sub-human situation, white slavery. If the worker dares to claim some improvement or some guarantee—to join a basic education course, a trade union, a co-operative—he is threatened with being turned off the land of the patriarch. If he persists, his house is demolished. If he tries to defend himself, he risks death. If he is beaten or assassinated, the family will not even have the consolation of seeing the crime punished, for in the underdeveloped regions the landowner is not only the master of life and death but he usually controls politics, the police and the frail structure of human justice.

—As for religion—I am referring here to Latin America (I do not know the position of the main religions in Africa and Asia, where there is internal colonialism)—as for christianity, regrettably it has kept its eyes firmly closed to the activities of the powerful and has connived at them. After having accepted the slavery of the Indians and African slavery, it has in practice accepted national slavery.

Wherever christianity today feels that it can no longer make alliances with such crying injustices, wherever it feels it cannot approve the situation in which a small group possesses everything, keeping millions of men in a sub-human situation; wherever it feels that the reform of socio-economic structures cannot be put off, christianity is opposed: the laity, priests and even bishops are labelled subversive and communist.

Furthermore, young people from the developed countries of the capitalist world, you must surely have noticed already that capitalist regimes create under-developed layers even in your own developed countries? The United States has had the courage to admit to the world that it has, within its own borders, thirty million Americans living in a situation unworthy of the human condition.

What developed country with a capitalist regime does not have its underdeveloped layers which, though on a different scale, share the poverty of the under-developed countries?

However, sadder still is the situation where, as in the United States, over and above material problems, racial prejudice breaks out, absurd and revolting. And this is the moment to bow to the memory of Pastor Martin Luther King who was coming to participate in our discussion and was assassinated.

We know that he conducted, in the United States, the non-violent battle undertaken by the Blacks, in order to obtain racial integration. It is the most beautiful, the most democratic and the most christian page in the contemporary history of the USA. Unfortunately the egoism of the Whites forces the Blacks to resort to violence, and it is to be feared that the holocaust of King—who fell like Gandhi, like Kennedy and like Christ himself—will inflame even more the hatred between Whites and Blacks, a hatred whose consequences are unforeseeable.

Young people of the developed capitalist countries, are you keeping an eye on the attitude of capitalism towards the underdeveloped countries? If we take as an example the relations between the United

States and Latin America, when one compares what Latin America receives in aid with what it loses in consequence of the falling prices of its raw materials; when one compares the money invested in Latin America with the money which returns to the United States (illegally, of course, but there are hundreds of ways of getting round it), one becomes aware of the nonsensical situation that it is Latin America which is aiding North America. And the same thing happens in the dealings between Asia and Africa and the developed countries.

The first UNCTAD took place and it was possible to raise a few hopes: the second took place and the hopes were dashed. We saw, more recently, how the Kennedy Round ended: by damaging the third world even more.

If, for capitalism, profit is the essential motor of economic progress, what can the underdeveloped countries expect from the capitalist countries, other than the crumbs which fall from the banqueting-tables? If, for capitalism, competition is the supreme law of the economy, the logical outcome is that, alongside pre-industrial societies, highly industrialised societies and even post-industrial societies will arise. If, for capitalism, private ownership is an absolute and sacred right, anticommunism and the defence of the free world are excellent pretexts for wars like the one in Vietnam, which scarcely bother to conceal a concern to maintain and extend zones of influence and of political prestige.

A fraternal message to the young people of the developed socialist countries

If capitalism arouses such grave reservations, and if it

81

leaves the impression of unavoidable internal contradictions, it has the merit of allowing the youth within its spheres of influence to be present here and join freely in the severe criticisms which we are making of the capitalist system.

However, if I am not mistaken, there are almost no young people here from developed socialist countries. What are the reasons for this absence, for this lack of dialogue? Is it a demonstration of the persistence of anti-religious prejudice on the part of socialism? Here much of the fault lies on our side too, since in practice we have become too involved with the capitalist mentality and are not really open to a dialogue with socialism?

But, in fact, there are faults on both sides. Theoretically, marxism defines itself as a humanism, indeed the only scientific humanism. Theoretically, socialism is based on profoundly human values: peace, solidarity and brotherhood between men, the emancipation of labour and, consequently, the setting up of a society of men truly free and equal.

In practice, socialism, under the pretext of defending itself from the capitalist regime, set up the Iron Curtain and the Wall of Shame. In practice, for decades the thoughts of Marx have been transformed into dogma, including his outlook on the alien and alienating essence of religion. This is the reason for militant atheism, religious persecution and, at best, the restriction of religious life exclusively to the inside of churches.

In practice, the class struggle continues, for the red dictatorship of the proletariat has not yet reached the paradisical phase lyrically predicted by Marx. The lack of creative liberty continues for artists and thinkers. The periodic purges continue within the Party itself, as well as the climate of distrust and denunciation.

When Hungary tried to use its own head and express its own feelings, we saw how it was crushed.

In practice, the USSR has satellites even more rigidly co-ordinated and controlled than the satellites of capitalist countries; the USSR, in meetings such as that of UNCTAD, adopts a position which is just as egoistic and reveals the same lack of understanding of the Third World as the United States; and the USSR and red China watch one another warily and fight just like two capitalist empires.

But none of this dispenses us christians from the very grave obligation of radically revising our attitude to marxism. Our experience of christianity in Latin America forces us to admit humbly that in practice we christians have often made religion the opium of the people and that we have been accomplices in the terrible injustices which still persist and which are crushing the masses of our continent.

Such errors on the part of christians led Marx to imagine that it was the very essence of the religion to be alien and alienating. At the moment when christianity, without forgetting transcendence, and preserving all the values of eternity, begins, in practice, to understand the lesson of the redeeming incarnation; to the degree in which we engage in reality; to the degree in which we admit, fearlessly, that God himself wished man to be an agent of history, giving him the mission of dominating nature and completing creation; to the degree in which christians cease once for all to work with any sort of economic or political regime whatever; to the degree above all in which this attitude of christians leads them to abandon the favours of the powerful and rulers, to be suspect, slandered and persecuted—more and more marxists will begin to look again at the concept of religion in general and the christian religion in particular.

Furthermore, all this coincides with the tendency to demythologise marxism and to make pluralism within the socialist system a reality. We all, for example, followed with interest and sympathy what happened in Czechoslovakia.

Without making the opposite mistake of tying christianity to socialism, would this not be an opportunity for young christians to invite the young people of the socialist countries to an open and fraternal dialogue, to examine what a revision in depth of socialism could mean for humanity, through profiting by its authentic values, liberating it from unjust, negative prejudices, bringing to it the unhoped-for and incomparable wealth of christian values?. . .

A fraternal message to the young people of the under-developed countries

All that has been said about capitalism and socialism has a direct repercussion on our countries of the third world.

What can I say, even more specifically, to the young people of the world to which I belong?

When, as a Latin American, I think of my under-developed brothers of Africa and Asia, I can see the terrible responsibility of christianity in Latin America.

When Africa and Asia met at Bandung, the need to

unite to survive in face of implacable imperialisms miraculously overcame the division of countless languages and the immense distances between extremely diverse religions. Now Latin America is practically one where language is concerned and the whole continent, at least in name, is christian. What a grave duty is ours, of being the seed of union in the third world!

Again a word to our brothers from the Third World: I fully understand your desire for violence. The injustices are too great and the coldness and unconcern of the powerful who exploit us are revolting. But wait and try to understand more fully this fraternal warning from someone who has experienced the sweat and dust of conflict: precisely because we are only interested in the cultural revolution and make no mistake about it: the structural revolution presupposes, necessarily, the cultural revolution.

A final message to the young people of the two hemispheres

To the young of North and South, from the developed world and from the underdeveloped world, I ask permission to add a final message. If you asked me what I considered most valuable, most strong, most effective as ferment of cultural revolution, at the level of the structural revolution of which the world is in need, I would answer without hesitation: authentic christianity, such as emerged from Vatican II. If you wish for a leader who, better than anyone, is capable of understanding the young and incapable of deceiving them, I would answer fearlessly: Christ!

85

8
The true greatness
of the USA

Lecture at Harvard, January 1969.

Problem No. 1

Harvard is certainly one of the four or five best universities in the USA. Hence my concern to profit by my
visit to Harvard to discuss with you a theme worthy of
the place and of the responsibility entrusted to you, in
your country, in your continent, in the world.

I suggest that we examine together the very topical
phenomenon of the relations between the armed forces
and the university.

Is this a subject for hope or one for alarm? Who is
likely to gain by this dialogue? Is it the university,
which is necessarily marked by the militarist spirit, or
is there a hope for the university of leading the armed
forces to more wholesome thinking?

May the Pentagon forgive my incursion into a field
which apparently belongs to it: it so happens that, for
one thing, the armed forces–university dialogue is not
the monopoly of the USA and, for another, the dialogue
taking place here has profound echoes, especially in
Latin America.

There are those who end up believing that the military are more like robots than human creatures—a grave mistake. Under the uniform, the military man conserves the same human body, the same human soul, with its almost infinite possibilities and its incurable frailty of Icarus and of Prometheus.

The American dream

Let me tell you how I view your country. The origin of your people and of your country seems to me of a surprising moral beauty. In short, what did the pilgrims who left old England claim? Freedom for their own religion, freedom to build a democracy which would perhaps serve as an example to other countries. They did not measure the sacrifices. They repeated the gesture of Abraham and, later, that of Moses, who abandoned all and left at the call of the Lord. And God rewarded them by giving them a land of promise, where milk and honey flowed.

Far be it from me to belittle the heroism your ancestors had to show. I do not wish to leave the impression here of believing naively that everything was freely given to you, instead of being won with great difficulty. Nevertheless it is indisputable that, without forgetting the immense efforts, there is a lot of Canaan in the land you have won.

You grew to such an extent that during the first world war Europe sent you an SOS appealing to you to save civilisation. You came, you saw, you conquered and you went away humbly, bringing with you the beautiful dream of Wilson, later realised in the UNO of today.

At the time of the second world war, a new anguished appeal. And, for the second time, you saved humanity. This time, you did not go away altogether: besides the military presence, the troops and bases, there was the Marshall Plan, which has been described as the most generous gesture ever made by a victor, made without prejudice to its important, and perhaps serious, commercial implications.

Is it surprising that after having been called twice to save the world, the wine has gone to your head a little? The reasoning of the military seems simple: if the world lacks good sense; if, in a century, the world has twice erupted, demanding of you, both times, extremely difficult improvisations and unparalleled sacrifices, perhaps it is better to maintain a discreet vigilance and a certain control over the world.

The gravest thing is that military victories open the way to commercial victories. When the second world war ended, England, as an empire, was gravely stricken. Leadership in trade passed into your hands. It is true that in 1939 an awkward ally arose: the USSR. Fortunately, here would be an excellent pretext for blocking its imperialist pretensions: it would be easy to appeal to the need to block the march of communist expansion in the world. The arms race began. The cold war came. Episodes followed, such as the war in Korea and the terrible, endless war in Vietnam.

During this time, the other empire was also moving. It advanced rapidly, to the point of covering a good third of the world with the hammer and sickle.

As long as it only involved Europe, this was disquieting but not intolerable, even when poignant chapters arose such as the crushing of the Hungarian revolt, an anticipation of the recent crushing of Czechoslovakia.

However, when the Russian bear turned towards Latin America, you jumped: for you thought you had a right to a direct zone of influence or, to put it more euphemistically, to a zone of security. And Cuba was harassed by the economic blockade and by the continental excommunication you imposed on all Latin America.

When, in an unforgettable moment, the USSR had the audacity to think of implanting on Cuban soil—in Latin American territory—a missile base, the world, for twenty-four hours, saw itself threatened with nuclear war. When a second Cuba began to take shape in the Dominican Republic, you went further than a simple economic blockade.

When you became aware that the guerillas were rising like an embodiment of hope for some Latin American groups and like an arm of expansion of the socialist empire, with the help of Cuba, you increased the number of anti-guerilla groups in the Latin American hemisphere and, today, the green berets are practically annulling the dream of the companions of Che Guevara.

A new surprise is emerging in red China: a surprise for the two empires who are throwing off, more and more, any pretext of ideological divergences and which, tomorrow, will make possible and easy and—who knows?—necessary, the USA–USSR pact against the third empire.

During this time, the USSR and the USA have persisted in failing to understand the true dimensions of the drama of the underdeveloped world, the so-called third world (Latin America, Africa and Asia). They continue to reason in terms of financial aid and technical assistance when the problem, fundamentally, is justice in international trade.

As I am not telling you anything new and only touching rapidly on the essential lines of a gigantic, dramatic and perhaps tragic history, you will certainly recall how these events have, each more than the last, consolidated the Pentagon, inevitably drawing it closer to economic power and political power.

Technological competition, vital just as much in the military domain as in the commercial, and essential for the space race, has of necessity imposed an alliance between the armed forces and the universities.

Before reminding the North American universities, through Harvard, of the terrible responsibility which, at this moment and under this aspect, weighs on the universities in the country of Abraham Lincoln, allow me to point out the main repercussions on Latin America of this situation which has grown up and which, day after day, is growing worse in that part of the world.

Repercussions in Latin America

It is easy to understand why, for your part, if you look at the atlas, you consider Latin America as an integral part of your defence system and, from the point of view of those responsible for the defence of the Latin American regions, an alliance with you seems normal, necessary and indispensable.

This is why one so often hears the phrases: 'we have embarked on the same adventure', 'we have the same common destiny'; 'what is in the interests of the USA is also in the interests of Latin America'....

This is why there are common programmes of socio-economic and politico-cultural development—but, above all, joint continental defence plans.

Your training in research teaches you not to let yourself be taken in by appearances, but to try to penetrate the kernel of what forms the object of the research.

What must Latin America think, what must it conclude, faced with facts you are more aware of than I and of which I remind you by offering a mere sample:

—the five biggest North American enterprises (General Motors, Ford, Standard Oil, General Electric and Chrysler) had in 1965 a turnover of about $55,255,000,000, almost seven times more than the total amount of the budgets for the same year of Brazil, the Argentine, Mexico, Chile, Venezuela and Colombia which, together, scarcely totalled the sum of $8,177,000,000.

Must we accept our vocation to be colonies and choose to keep in the shadow of your democratic and christian empire rather than run the risk of transferring to the orbit of socialism, which crushes the human person and erases the idea of God?

Will the Latin American continental security system have to welcome the crumbs that fall from your table and gratefully receive the arms which are out of date for you but which serve well enough to defend our Latin American governments, whether democratic or dictatorial, just or arbitrary, progressive or connected with local oligarchies?

Does capitalism or even neo-capitalism truly respect the human person? Is it not its very essence to consider profit as the supreme goal, even if this means crushing human creatures?

Let us go on to the accusations of the first and second UNCTAD: when one compares the aid received by the underdeveloped countries with what they lose in consequence of the depreciation in price of their raw materials, and when one compares US investments in Latin America with the money which returns (thanks to facilities created for dollar investments and by many devices, more or less illegal), one becomes aware that the absurd is taking place: it is underdeveloped Latin America, it is the continent of thousands of 'marginals', which is giving aid to the North American giant.

God forbid that we should judge intentions, particularly of a man of the moral stature of John Kennedy. But today, before God, he would be the first to recognise that the Alliance for Progress has been, from its origin, an instrument falling far short of his dreams and above all, he would see how his generous and statesmanlike gesture has been twisted and disfigured.

I do not think that the solution lies in increasing aid, doubling or tripling it. Nor is it to impose on us a remote-controlled policy of birth control. The solution is much more complex and much more difficult: it entails a radical revision of international trade policies.

The text of the Alliance for Progress laid down as condition for receiving aid that there should be reform of the socio-economic and political-cultural structures responsible for internal colonialism in Latin America, i.e. those responsible for the presence of a tiny minority of privileged whose wealth is maintained at the expense of millions of fellow Latin Americans.

Quite often when, in some country or other of Latin America, someone decides to undertake a real change in structures, the privileged cry out and label it subversion of the social order and communism. The local governments get alarmed and the USA worries in the background, for it is in no way in their interests for any government to arise which tomorrow may degenerate into a second Cuba. But by so doing, they maintain and perpetuate a situation which, itself, crushes the human person.

The Latin American Catholic hierarchy, which met at Medellin under the direct chairmanship of the Holy Father, did not hesitate to call it sub-human and compromising to peace.

The understanding of the nation

You may ask me: why should the armed forces intervene in the face of such widespread and complex problems? In particular, you may ask what is the role of the university.

There exists today a philosophy personified by the Pentagon and communicated to the armies of all the countries under the influence of the USA. To the degree in which this philosophy is purified of errors and prejudices which make it one-sided and dangerous, there will be hope of overcoming neo-colonialism and of marching together towards a harmonious and cooperative development of peoples.

Now, in this effort to reformulate the political philosophy which is at the basis of all the foreign policy of the USA and of every programme of continental security, the university has a mission which it can only ignore at the risk of betraying humanity.

There is no question of chance: it is not by chance that the armed forces are drawing nearer to the university. You know, and there is no need for me to repeat it to you, that you bear the responsibility of being the intelligence of your country.

Allow me to name a few points which, dealt with at university level by Harvard and its American counterparts, would have the most beneficial world repercussions:

1. Help the USA to take up an ever clearer and more courageous position in the clashes between empires, so that ideological reasons are not invoked when, at bottom, the interests are economic ones.

2. Help the USA to not carry too far its messianic role as controller of the world, guardian of democracy and of basic human rights.

3. Help the USA to understand that the best way of stimulating democracy is to respect it, in an effective and total way, within its own frontiers and in its international relations.

4. Help the USA to understand that development is the new name for peace and that without justice there will be no development. A decisive measure would be that of transforming the Alliance for Progress into the Alliance for Justice and Peace.

5. Help the USA to speed up structural changes by setting an example and seriously examining the possibilities of a change in its own internal structures, and realising that, in relation to the changes in the third world, far from fearing that these changes can give rise to the infiltration of communism, nothing will precipitate the underdeveloped countries into subversion and radicalism faster than their remaining in a situation of poverty and subhumanity;

6. Help the USA not to fear the education of the masses, human development, community organisation. Authentic democracy and true christianity can only rejoice at such movements. To treat them as subversion and communism is to make communist propaganda.

7. Help the USA to look again at the concepts of capitalism and socialism. Help them to discover a personalist socialisation which does not involve dictatorship by government or party and creates a climate of expansion for the human person and the community.

8. Help the USA to contribute, in a decisive way, to the reformation of the United Nations, so that it can avoid discriminations between great and small powers, integrate courageously the whole human family and become the organisation foreseen by John XXIII and dreamt of by Paul VI.

9. Help the USA to give the example of revision of military power while erasing once for all the impression that it is to the military that the mission of super-government and super-technicians falls, and courageously predicting the discovery of another essential aim for a military career, now that wars are becoming more and more absurd, more inhuman and more immoral.

10. Help the USA to show the world how man can advance boldly in the fields of science and technology, without in any way claiming to do without God or become a God.

May your country, born of the decision of fidelity to Christ, be the living testimony that the God-Man is the only answer to our thirst for divinisation.

Part 3

The necessary revolution

9
The mission of the universities

A lecture given at the Catholic University of Chile, April 1969.

The era of the Third World

My meeting with Chile and the Catholic University of Santiago takes place at an exceptional historical moment for the Third World. At the end of the first development decade, humanity has admitted that it has not done anything much. Last year at New Delhi our representatives at UNCTAD drew up the balance-sheet of our set-backs. Latin America, as part of the Third World, has a duty to find new paths of development. The efforts of the peoples of the continent, their capacities for creation, their organised and conscious activities and their energy can overcome the dependence and the alienation which exist at the moment in various forms. How can we discuss the problem of development today without drawing in all the implications of economic, political and cultural dependence? And how can this state of affairs be overcome without expressing our reality? How can this be done without a social theory inspired by the originality of our culture and at the same time open to a critical assimilation of general scientific development?

This is the context in which we have to see the historical role of the Latin American universities. It is not a matter of asking for a dialogue between the university and the society around it, as though they were completely separate. The university forms part of society and is the expression of it, or, more precisely, it should be, in the process of transformation, its critical conscience. It cannot remain indifferent to the surrounding society, of which it is the expression at the level of culture, as both the achievement of the past and the seed of the future. The university can decide either to be an expression of the present structures and become the support of the status quo, or to try and express the consciousness of a society looking towards the future. On the other hand, a university which reforms itself only has meaning in a society which is itself changing; the university foreshadows and anticipates the changes in society. Will our universities have the imagination and the daring to prepare for the world of tomorrow, or will they choose to remain a relic of the past? The restless presence of the young reassures me on this point. They already foreshadow this anticipation of tomorrow.

Revolutions vital to development

1. *Technological revolution*

Which aspects of the reality of our continent could benefit most from a creative contribution on the part of our universities? Allow me to present to you here some points which, even though they do not exhaust all the perspectives, at least offer us some suggestions.

The present demands of the economic, political and social revolutions which the development of Latin America entails are bound up with the scientific and technical revolution, in which the universities obviously have a decisive role to play. It is important to direct the present priorities of scientific studies systematically and intensely towards the problems of contemporary science which are most relevant to the needs and the aspirations of man in this underdeveloped part of the continent.

We must see that we shall not detract from academic dignity or the greatness of the university by devoting the facilities and opportunities for scientific research as a matter of priority to overcoming the present situation of general, institutionalised poverty. This means not just choosing the objects of scientific research according to this criterion, but, more important, ensuring that they find immediate and effective application; it is a matter of promoting a growth, both autonomous and sustained by the whole of the Latin American economies, which would be the bearer of an authentic reform of structures capable of assuring the redistribution and the growth of incomes.

The present scientific deficiencies of our technology make it an import with characteristics by and large inadequate to the solution of our own economic problems. Sometimes—as is happening in the considerable effort being made to overcome the underdevelopment of the Brazilian North East—the methods of production chosen are inadequate to create sufficient jobs. This is due to the fact that, without exception, a technology is adopted which is intensive but not very productive of jobs; hence, an unemployed labour force is growing daily larger; or again the imported elements in a region do not take advantage of its rare economic factors. Consequently we have to create a technology or adapt it to the specific requirements of a region. But this cannot be done without a basis of scientific research at a high and systematic level. A revolution is needed to change academic attitudes and habits in order to orientate the scientific and technological effort of the universities towards the urgent tasks of development.

Such an effort could be translated into changes of programmes and into projects which, once set going, would be the instruments for bringing about development. Of course these instruments can be used in different and even opposite ways and can have very different effects on human development. Such a transformation can be yet another modernisation of the processes of production, and be appropriated yet again by better-off social groups. In such a neo-capitalist spirit, technical progress will make too little, or even no contribution at all to the real development of the masses at present deprived.

This shows how any kind of transformation, whether technological or economic, must of necessity be based on a more general view which takes account of socio-political factors.

2. Political revolution

To prevent the drain of qualified human resources, we must take measures to keep in Latin America our qualified human resources, who, today, are going to the developed countries, as though we were running a programme of technical aid to them. From 1960 to

1965, to take the medical field as an example, over three thousand professionals permanently emigrated from Latin America to the United States. This represents an estimated overall loss, for the Latin American countries, of 60 million dollars.

But to find solutions one must go to the root of the problems. As long as the élite are not from the people and do not express it in a critical way, they will not feel involved with the people. In order to make them remain in the country, it is not enough to offer them better living and working conditions; the gap will remain and the élite will continue to leave for other countries, as long as there is no democratisation of education. A university which is not of the people is destined to form instruments of domination, of internal and external colonialism.

The most evident political fact of our continent is the absence of popular participation in decision-making. This means, in other words, that the people do not share in the political process, either because there are no authentic popular consultations, because a section of the people does not vote, or again because of lack of interest: abstention where popular consultation exists, apathy towards the regimes where this is excluded. Is one of the reasons that the decisions taken do not correspond to the real problems of the people? Do we not lack the courage to undertake the rapid and profound transformations which are necessary in order to get to the very roots of this problem?

It can also be that the efforts to allow the working class and peasant population benefit from the social transformations are useless, because such efforts have been undertaken without genuine participation and

103

without the fruits of their work being given them. This fact would seem to demand a search for alternative models which can courageously promote real changes in the structures of production and in the structure of power. This structural change would immediately involve the institutional body which supports the unjust privileges which distort the distribution of the fruits of human labour. Secondly, it would involve all aspects of the organisation of economic activity, from the management of firms, where there has to be participation by all those concerned with production, to the distribution of products.

How can the university participate in this new type of popular presence and anticipate it without being open to this people and to its needs, and allowing it to exercise its responsibilities? How can the university begin to think of the democratisation of society if it does not begin by being itself a democratic community capable of working out its own problems and those of its country? Here I think I can see another important contribution a reformed university could make.

It is not enough for the people to participate in the internal structures of power; at the international level our countries must have a real share in the process of world decision-making. How far are the great powers ready to accept this? It is up to us in any case to create instruments of communication, to organise ourselves into pressure groups and to acquire the competence which will make other nations listen to us. What a responsibility awaits the Latin American universities, to prepare this dialogue in dimensions which are today not only worldwide but probably already cosmic!

On the other hand, the contribution of the university to economic, technological and political transformations will only have meaning if it is integrated into a broader context of cultural transformation, where its contribution will be specific and still more decisive.

3. *Cultural revolution*

Are we not faced with a cultural revolution such as is desired by the young of the whole world? To change our society signifies a break with the system of bourgeois values founded on egoism and individual success. Is not what we are questioning today the way in which men establish relationships, both among themselves and with the world? There is much talk today of the end of humanism and the death of man. Man is not dying today in the abstract speculation of thinkers but, more concretely, through lack of bread and knowledge. Are we not seeing today the death of man in general, or more precisely of a certain way of being man, in a humanity divided among those who possess all they want and those who have scarcely anything they need?

To overcome this situation by social transformations, shall we not have to look for new means of expression, a new humanism, for the coming decade? If the sixties were disappointing in the field of development, could the seventies not become the years of human liberation? A movement of liberating pressure would have to rediscover the very image of man, fashioned in the likeness of God. Where can this be done if not in a permanent encounter between the people, who represent the forgotten man, and the university, which seeks him in its theoretical reflection? Man is reborn when action and thought unite to redeem him.

Have we made an effort to discover all the possibilities for a meeting between popular culture and university knowledge? More concretely, must not the knowledge of a university which is trying to free itself from its alienation begin with what the people are creating? This discovery will not be possible unless the people become aware of their unsuspected potentialities. Does not this meeting allow us to rediscover ourselves on the basis of our needs and of an identity which has remained hidden?

This is a task proper to the whole of Latin America, united as it is by common historical and cultural ties. I find it very significant that a university which has decided to be at the very heart of national reality, and which in order to do so has created a special unit, has also decided to extend its studies to the whole Latin American reality. And when we say the whole of Latin America we cannot exclude any country. Something will always be lacking in our continent until we have reintegrated Cuba and its socio-political experience into our community of nations. Nor may we forget the emerging countries of the Caribbean, who are linked with us by our common social problems, even though we may speak different languages.

Today, Latin America, including Cuba, is meeting at Lima to discuss a common strategy. It is significant that the country where the representatives of Latin America are meeting is Peru, where the challenge of the relationship between the underdeveloped countries and the developed countries appears most sharply. Nor is it a matter of making a simple analysis of the present. Let us have the imagination to think ahead in to the future and the desire to do so in a more human way.

Conclusions

I have already told you that I came to Chile more to learn than to teach. These happy days shared with you have given me the chance to talk to professors, students, and in particular with the Rector. I discovered there more fully the spirit guiding your university reform.

Let us imagine that after these dialogues I was asked how I found the Catholic university of Santiago. Here, before you, as though for an examination which would serve to evaluate what I have learned, I shall dare to tell you the points which I found striking and which I saw to be the centre of your preoccupations:

1. Your university has not created an abstract model outside of history, nor a naive copy of other models, but has tried to discover a path at the very heart of the culture into which it was born and in which it is living; it is thus a university involved in Chilean reality.
2. You do not regard this reality as something given but as something which is in the process of formation, and thus you make the university a centre for examining the process.
3. This criticism develops on the basis of a pluralism open to choice and to different trends.
4. For this, you have created an active participation of professors and students, in a community of work and research.
5. All this will be possible only if the people are regarded as the actual subject of the historical process.

Then the different functions of research, reflection and creation, teaching, professional training and services to the local and national community will develop in a critical dialogue with the people.

6. These demands, as well as making us discover the cultural process, make us denounce anything imposed from outside which has claimed the right to make us accept rules and models in the economic, social, political and above all in the cultural field.

7. This engagement with the reality of your country is one of the best translations of the profound humanist sense which animates christianity.

8. And it is at the very heart of Chilean reality that you meet the universal element which transcends frontiers and that your experience becomes a source of inspiration for other universities by opening broader horizons for them.

All these points are in agreement with the document prepared during the episcopal meeting at Buga, as well as with the texts of the CELAM meeting at Medellin. At Buga, the bishops present defined the university as 'the consciousness of the historical process, where the past becomes present in the creation of new forms of culture'. And the text continues—I shall quote the most significant passages: 'This consciousness of the culture is manifested in knowledge, institutionalised in the university community which, through a permanent dialogue of its members among one another and with society, participates in the personalisation and in the socialisation of man in a world which is changing and becoming more human'.

And further on it states: 'All the particular and permanent tasks of the university, such as, among others, research and the training of staff, must be integrated while remaining faithful to the demands of discipline, in reflection on the process of liberation; for this a close contact with the sources and forms of popular culture is indispensable.

'With this aim, the university must provide conditions which allow its members to exercise in a critical way their responsibility of participation in the political process, with a view to the common good. In this sense, we envisage the necessary politicisation of the members of the university community.

'It is also of capital importance for the university institution to make an effort to seek out elements capable of promoting in a continuous way the cultural independence of the people from forms of submission coming from inside or outside. The liberation sought must be the root of a fruitful integration, both of individuals in society, and of the Latin American societies in a common effort.'

These are the words of the bishops at Buga.

At Medellin, the whole Latin American episcopate, through its delegates, made this criticism: 'Our universities have not taken sufficiently into consideration the particular characteristics of Latin America; by frequently taking over models from the developed countries, they have not given an adequate answer to the particular problems of our continent. Latin America needs a liberating education to redeem itself from unjust servitude and, most of all, from our own egoism. This is the education demanded by a total development.' Further on, the bishops declare: 'As any liberation is in itself an anticipation of the total redemption of Christ, the church of Latin America feels particularly at one with any educative effort which helps to liberate our peoples.'

My dear friends: will all this remain a dream? Will it remain a vague hope, a fantasy born of this festive evening, as ephemeral as a firework? Not at all!

I have crossed the Cordillera to tell you: go on! Do not let what is natural and necessary frighten those about you, endangering the efforts of all. Whoever lights a torch of hope has not the right to let it go out! I say this not to feed any vanity, but so that you can gauge your responsibility fully: Latin America is watching you.

10
Atomic hope

Speech to students of the engineering school at the federal university of Rio de Janeiro, November 1967.

Professional outlook for an atomic engineer

You will certainly have already noticed that in our era, when man is becoming aware of his divine mission of mastering nature and completing creation, the engineer—the artisan par excellence of nature—has powers of good and evil. He can become an instrument for the humanisation or the dehumanisation of the world.

I should like to consider the need for an ethic for the modern engineer and in particular for a professional code for the atomic engineer.

Don't worry: this is not going to be a moralising sermon. If there are engineers who make napalm bombs and who construct dehumanising blocks of flats, if there are others who work, consciously or otherwise, for the levelling-down and reification of man— for my part I am with those who still believe in the human person. And I am sure that in the field of this profession good will triumph, through the power of divine grace.

The code of the atomic engineer would be above all the awareness of the almost unbelievable powers placed at his disposal. It must involve the voluntary and sacred commitment to use such creative powers only for the profound transformation of the physiognomy of the country and of the continent. And this must be done for the happiness of all Brazilians and of all Latin Americans, in an effort to keep at the same time an openness towards the other underdeveloped continents, and a concern for the harmonious development of the world.

1. *Science fiction?*

When one hears for the first time of the peaceful use of atomic energy, one's immediate reaction is negative. And this is explained by the following objections:

—Atomic explosions for peaceful ends? Is it not, for example, madness to wish Brazil to enter the Nuclear Bomb Club?

—The peaceful use of nuclear energy? But who can assure us that even half of the marvels demanded will be obtained, such as the cutting of canals, of ports, the boring of mines, the linking of river networks, all these projects which seem utopian?

—The peaceful use of the atom? It is bound to take a long time before Brazil has sufficient assets for such projects.

Nevertheless, one after the other these objections fail: The super-powers accuse the underdeveloped countries of lacking a sense of responsibility; the latter, under the pretext of the peaceful use of nuclear energy, could employ it to unleash war.

The accusation is so insulting that it does not merit an answer. It is enough to recall that, if we wished, we could have full access to a bacteriological war or to a gas war: such tragic plans have never entered our imagination.

It is a curious and revolting thing: we are accused of irresponsibility, on the one hand by those who abuse power to maintain whole peoples behind the Iron Curtain, and on the other hand by those who irresponsibly force their young people to die without glory, committing atrocities which bring dishonour on the human race.

Furthermore, we Brazilians know quite well that we have not and will not have full maturity where war is concerned. To tell the truth, our past is not all that reassuring for some of our neighbours. And as for the future, there will be no lack of bad Brazilians who could nourish more or less veiled imperialist dreams. But we have confidence in the youth of Brazil, that new country in the process of being born, more mature and richer in responsible culture.

To the fantastic accusation that Brazil wants to race ahead in the technological battle, we reply that it is an illusion to believe that we are a sub-race, because we are half-breeds. And then, to present the peaceful use of atomic energy as a dream, because it would involve astronomical costs, is to forget that peaceful nuclearisation would reduce to a fifth the costs normally involved.

Finally, the most serious objection: is not the hope

placed in the peaceful use of nuclear energy exagge-
rated, ridiculous, naive?

2. *Arguments for the sceptical*

How can one evaluate what the peaceful use of nuclear
energy can achieve and offer humanity?

Let us look at what the USA has been doing since
1957.

The famous Plowshare Plan dates from this time.
We shall refer to this for evidence of projects demanded
either by the North American government or by some
of the biggest companies of the United States. When
the economic powers are activated and distribute
dollars widely, no Thomas can obviously continue to
remain sceptical.

The Plowshare Plan foresees the possibility of resort-
ing to atomic explosion to cut canals. In 1964, President Johnson authorised studies for the construction,
in Panama, of another canal at sea level, using atomic
energy. Even if one is still waiting in 1968 for decisive
information, it is already known that the cost of the
Sassardi-Norti project, in Eastern Panama, was estimated at 747 million dollars, using nuclear explosives.
The same project would cost 2,280 million dollars if
traditional methods were used.

'Geonuclear Corporation' is the name given to a
commercial organisation formed in Las Vegas. The
total of twenty-four American petroleum companies
comprising this corporation got together specifically
to study, within the framework of the Plowshare Plan,
the extraction of bituminous schist. According to the
text of the technical report, an underground nuclear
explosion disintegrates the schist, which is subsequently
set alight. After this, the distillation of the petroleum is

114

carried out by hot air pressure through the disintegrated mass.

The Natural Gas Company of El Paso was interested in 1968—again within the Plowshare Plan—in a nuclear explosion to get at the deposits of natural gas in deep and less permeable rock formations. A report demonstrated the technical and economic feasibility of the project: it was evaluated that the same deposits, producing by the use of traditional methods 10% of gas over twenty years, could produce 90% using nuclear stimulants.

The Kennecott Corporation decided, after official authorisation, to use nuclear explosions in a copper stratum of low yield and situated at considerable depth, at Stafford, Arizona. Once the ore is disintegrated, an injection of sulphuric acid into the pit dissolves the copper and forces it to the surface.

The Santa Fé Railroad plans to use a nuclear explosion to make a railway cutting in the Bristol Mountains (California).

It would be easy to add to the examples of powerful organisations practically engaged in fantastic enterprises utilising nuclear energy for peaceful ends. In all these cases, the price of nuclear energy is much lower than normal prices. And to conclude, yet another example: in the Chariot project, for the opening of a port at Cape Thompson (Alaska), the price of excavation per cubic yard with nuclear apparatus ($0·55) is lower than that of traditional excavation ($2–$5).

This is why there are so many projects in the Plowshare Plan, ranging from the desalination of water to the clearing of navigable waterways, from the opening of roads to the linking of river systems.

3. *The peaceful use of the atom*

The statement made by the Military High School is very true: 'We have lost the coal age; we arrived late in the petroleum age; we cannot afford the luxury of being late in the nuclear age.'

The advantage is that we are not starting out from zero in this sector. However limited the outlay of Brazil in the field of research (between 0·21 and 0·28% of the gross national product), we nevertheless already have three Institutes of Nuclear Research: the Institute of Atomic Energy in Sao Paulo, the Institute of Radioactive Research in Belo Horizonte, and the Institute of Nuclear Energy in Rio de Janeiro.

In spite of the terrible precariousness of means, research is going ahead, with encouraging results. Here is a typical example: in the Maranhao-Piaui basin, which is of sedimentary nature, aerial prospecting, using the scintillometer (a device for measuring the radiations of uranium and thorium) has already indicated 420 areas where radiations are at quite a high level.

The Brazilian people must be persuaded that an underdeveloped country is by no means synonymous with irresponsibility, and that economic power is not, ipso facto, synonymous with responsibility. We must believe in ourselves: as much in our capacity for victory in the technological battle as in our having the good sense to avoid the madness of a nuclear war.

We must ask the government for massive investment for research, and particularly for atomic research. A serious nuclear policy is necessary, within the framework of a national plan, and an appeal to the capacity of all Brazilians, without any political or ideological discrimination. And this will be a proof of our maturity. A child cannot play with fire, and especially with this sort of fire. We must be adults in word and deed.

Let us show ourselves capable of promoting, in this Polytechnic School, the speciality of the twentieth century: geographical and nuclear genius.

4. *The peaceful use of the atom and the Third World*
The conquest of the Amazon seemed a dream in former times, just as the battle of the North-East and of the Central-West.

What will the Brazilian Plan for the peaceful use of the atom be called? What will this plan be called, born here, by Brazilian efforts, in contact with our own reality and under the impulse of a love which urges us to drag millions of Brazilians out of a sub-human situation?

It is impossible to remain egoistic and mean when one realises the immense perspectives the engineering profession opens to the spirit of man. Never before has man, created in the image and likeness of God, been able to grasp the scope of such powers, which make him a co-creator. We must reason in continental terms.

The engineers of Brazil must join their colleagues of Latin America and, as soon as possible, work out the geographical basis of the economic integration of the continent, through the crossing of mountains, the linking of rivers, the construction of ports, the desalination of water, thus making previously uneconomic operations profitable. The engineers of Latin America must collaborate with their colleagues in Asia and Africa, in order to transform the face of the third world and speed the arrival of development.

5. *The peaceful use of nuclear power in Brazil*

The official declarations of the President of the Republic and the Foreign Minister demonstrate this to us in an indisputable way.

Allow me to remind you of a few points:

'Not yet freed from one form of underdevelopment, without nuclear energy we shall quickly fall into another, more dangerous one, that of science and technology. We must free ourselves from a situation in which we simply import foreign techniques and have constantly to pay 'royalties', the subjects of yet another form of slavery: the colonisation of the Atomic Age.

'We must free ourselves from our present economic and technological inferiority. We are engaged in a race against time. To develop must be for us synonymous with never letting up. The country must be mobilised for research. Priority task: the peaceful utilisation of nuclear energy.

'A country will only be truly independent and remain so if it does not resign itself to scientific neo-colonialism, and shows itself capable of developing its own technological solutions.

'A nation which is not convinced of this new reality will condemn itself inescapably to a state of subordination in politics as well, in which the payment of "royalties" will resemble the tributes exacted in former times by imperial powers.'

There is another quotation concerning the prohibition imposed by the super-powers on attempting nuclear explosions. This is an important point: 'To accept such a prohibition would reduce us to a situation similar in all respects to that decreed by the Queen of Portugal, Mary I, who forbade the establishment of iron foundries in Brazil.'

118

My presumption in dealing with such questions may astonish you. But what forces me to do so is solely the christian concern to be useful to the human person. The technological era is a two-edged sword. On the one hand, there is cold material domination, in which man becomes a cog, and the spirit the fruit of electronic brains. On the other hand there is the power of man to master the world to make it more human and help the human person to become more in possession of himself and more humane.

I wish that in the world of here and now intelligent men may perceive, through nuclear energy, the new dimension of the twenty-first century and that they may be ready to master it instead of being dominated by it.

In our country your profession has already given proof of its competence and daring. It has built three of the biggest hydro-electric dams in the world, Paulo Afonso, Furnas and Tres-Marias. It has built the Belem–Brasilia highway, under truly epic conditions. And in four years it has raised, in the heart of the Central-West, the capital of the future, Brasilia.

Start out on the road to peaceful nuclearisation, plunge fully into your profession as atomic engineers. But stamp your work, more and more, with a human meaning. It is not enough to create bold plans. Refuse to become mere instruments of high finance, which is in its turn subjugated to the international trusts. Consecrate your intelligence and your technical knowledge to the service of the total development of man and to that of the united development of humanity.

11
Ecumenical dialogue or permanent reformation

Speech at the theology faculty of the Methodist Church of Brazil, Sao Paulo, December 1967.

A gesture which is no longer unthinkable
Blessed be God, the Father of our Lord Jesus Christ, Father of mercy and God of all consolation. Thanks be to him for the joy of this night which would have been inconceivable for you and for us all a few years ago.

The ecumenical movement has received the breath of the divine Spirit; on the Protestant side was born the World Council of Churches; on the Catholic side, there was a man whose name was John, then the ecumenical council Vatican II was held, then came Paul VI.

Those who saw and heard, at the end of the council, in the Basilica of St Paul, Orthodox bishops and Anglican and Protestant clergy, united fraternally with the council fathers and with the pope, praying together to the Word of God, singing the praises of the Most High, received the best of motivations for an ever deeper and wider ecumenical dialogue.

And ecumenical gestures increase, spontaneously,

120

translating the fullness of understanding and love. To quote only the two greatest and most recent of these gestures, let us remember first of all how Paul VI gave his place on the throne of the Vatican Basilica to Patriarch Athenagoras in order that the latter might bless the Orthodox faithful who had come to receive the patriarchal blessing. And let us also recall the Pontifical Commission for Justice and Peace and the World Council of Churches which together called for an ecumenical meeting to unite more and more the efforts of the whole christian family to facilitate the paths of development. It is a profoundly christian concept, if we consider development as the new name for peace.

Let us then profit by the happiness of this fraternal encounter, and in homage to this great night let us meditate together on the responsibility and the joy of being christians. In Christ, we have the power and duty to extend:

—to our brothers surrounded by different types of atheism, the offer of a personal meeting with the Creator and Father;

—to our brothers in fear, bitter through hopelessness, on the brink of despair, the offer of a chance to plunge into the living and true hope;

—to our brothers who create in spite of the lack of love and who live in the harsh climate of division and hatred, the offer of a direct and personal initiation into the love of God and the love of men.

An unrecognised thirst for faith

1. *Meeting our atheist brothers*

The happiness and the responsibility of believing in

God and knowing that he cherishes us, leads us necessarily to dialogue with our atheist brothers.

Today atheism is no longer an unusual phenomenon, the way of life of a few rare, strange beings, but, in several huge areas of the world, a mass phenomenon. Today there exists an aggressive and militant atheism which tries to develop techniques for preventing the formation of belief in God and stamping it out of the lives of believers, just as there is beginning to be a passive atheism, which is simply an absence of God.

Consider in particular marxist atheists. It is easy to understand this position. If it is true that there are states dominated by marxism which still maintain a militant and aggressive atheism, there also exist marxist philosophers who are trying to lead christians and marxists from anathema to dialogue.

There is one fact which did not escape the marxist Roger Garaudy, even though it is probably rejected by many christians: if one third of humanity is christian and another third marxist, it is impossible to reorganise the world without christians, just as much as without marxists. As the age of dialogue has overcome that of anathema, we can and we must, without the slightest infidelity to our respective convictions, attempt a dialogue.

Garaudy discovers three trends in contemporary christian thought which enable christianity to be heard and understood by an atheist: the demythologisation of Rudolf Bultmann or of Bishop Robinson; the relation between religion and science as seen by Teilhard de Chardin; and the construction of the future as envisaged by the theologian Karl Rahner.

Certainly, both Catholics and Protestants make certain reservations about the exegetical work of Bultmann and his disciples, but the starting-point of de-mythologisation is common ground. God, even though he is the Father who wishes to be within reach of all his creatures, whom he raises to the rank of sons, none-theless was, is and will be an infinite and transcendent God, while we creatures were, are, and always will be finite and contingent creatures. Thus the Word of God, the basis and foundation of our faith, must inevitably be clothed in human dress.

How can the Creator and Father speak to us without adapting himself to our language, to our perception, to our culture, to our limitations? Even when revela-tion reached its apogee and the true Son of God was made man and lived among us, he had to accept the humiliation of depending on one region, one culture and one language.

Those who look at family albums and smile at the fashions of yesterday will easily understand the need to dress according to the fashions of the day. But with eternal truths which must accompany us on the whole of our journey, the problem is even more serious: the bond between the idea and the expression which trans-lates it is deeper than the simple relation between body and clothing. A moment comes when the human in-telligence rejects the expressions of yesterday, not only as being out of date, but more often as being unsuit-able and inadequate. Since we were created in the image and likeness of God, there is no reason for surprise that as men we are always advancing and that it is always possible for us to go further and see further, more clearly, and more deeply. Nor is there any need, even in this delicate and difficult prob-lem, to warn us of the dangers of attempts to reach the essential of the divine message, in freeing it of old-fashioned clothing and in trying to express it in a more suitable way. If it were simply a question of theological formulation, we could still, with relative ease, understand each other. But what value is a theology which is not based on scripture and which does not in itself develop, live and grow? Could we then have the courage to grasp the Word of God? What is to be done? Should we retain unwarranted innovations? Is there a work of renewal to be carried out? To reassure ourselves, we need only remember that we are not abandoned and alone. In the last resort, does the church belong to us or to Christ? Who guides it? We or the Holy Spirit? Have the gates of Hell begun to prevail against her?

On the Protestant side as on the Catholic side there are reservations about the thought of Teilhard de Chardin—but where is the theologian who does not arouse reservations? It appears, in short, perfectly possible for christian thought to envisage the Creation as an evolution and to accept that, in the plan of God, man, created in his image and likeness, the moment he emerges, receives the task of dominating nature and of completing creation.

The marxist who has come to regard the Bible with attention and respect is seduced by christianity's idea of man as the creator of history.

Rahner declares christianity to be the religion of the absolute future. 'If man progresses, if there is a true history, this is due to the evidence of an absolute, transcendent plenitude, which propels the human project forwards.

'Because this active and demanding presence exists in every man, he can, submerged in his history, transcend it and surpass it.

'Atheism is born when man no longer recognises God in this appeal, but confuses his absolute future with a concrete future. To recognise God in the absolute future of man is to make an integral humanism possible.'

The marxist recognises the never satisfied demand of the totality of the absolute. But he believes that his thirst is not a proof of the existence of the source. To transform the anguished questions into replies would be for him a religious alienation. Garaudy asks: 'Would it not be impoverishing man to teach him that he is an incomplete being, when everything depends on him, all our history and its meaning develop in the intelligence of man, in his heart and in his will, and nowhere else?'

To this, he himself replies: 'I believe that the marxist atheist allows man the illusion of uncertainty. I believe that the marxist dialectic, lived fully, is in the end infinitely richer and more demanding than christian transcendence.'

Unfortunately, our christian witness is more often a cause for scandal than a confirmation for us in the faith, it drives people from religious practice and—who knows?—from religious belief.

Imagine what it would mean for the marxist:

—to discover a religion which had nothing alien or alienating about it, a christianity incarnate like Christ himself;

—to have the surprise of seeing christians who, far from imagining a mean God, jealous of man, present a great and generous God, who rejoices to see man displaying powers capable of shaking the universe, of 'planting stars', and of being on the point of dominating life;

—to meet christians just as severe as themselves in their analysis of the immorality of a system which considers profit as the essential force of economic progress, competition as the supreme law of the economy, the ownership of the means of production as an absolute right;

—to know that christianity did not depend on any political regime, was not attached to any economic system, to any literary school, or any scientific hypothesis;

—to realise that, in practice, and tomorrow, God willing, in theory there exists and will exist the christian freedom to accept, from among the different types of socialism, those which will allow and encourage the flowering of the human person and community development.

Imagine what it will mean for our atheist brothers—marxist and non-marxist—to feel that religion is for us a life, that God is for us a reality in which we live, and move, and have our being; that to live not only before God, but in God, far from removing us from men, makes us truly brothers of all; far from tearing us from the earth, leads us to exercise fully our mission of mastering nature and completing the creation; far from making us sad, makes us full and happy creatures!

Who knows but that our example of faith might not draw them to God!

2. *Meeting our brothers who have given up hope*
It is difficult, indeed very difficult, to be an authentic christian surrounded by our brothers marked by

126

despairs of a material nature—and over two-thirds of humanity, as we know, is vegetating in a sub-human situation or fighting to escape from underdevelopment and hunger; among brothers marked by moral despairs —and, more often, comfort and luxury, far from bringing peace and giving joy, create discouragement and bitterness—in a world shared between the sub-life of the poor, with all its bitterness, and the inhuman superlife of the rich, we christians are not of a different nature from anyone else. We run the same risks as our brothers in humanity.

On the other hand, wherever we live, in us our non-christian or non-religious brothers must encounter a testimony of hope.

Those of us who are poor must try to live with humility the hopes which are not fulfilled; to struggle tirelessly and unflinchingly; to confront the real situation sensibly, without alienation and without flight; to be an example of courage when discouragement is overpowering all; to give heart again when an impasse is reached, to conquer resentments, bitterness and hatred. And to do all this without believing oneself the most powerful or most strong, but overflowing with a hope which has once and for all taken possession of our souls, for Jesus Christ is risen.

Those of us who are rich must try to avoid insensitivity, in ourselves and towards our surroundings. It is often easy for rich people to wear blinkers, which make it impossible for them to discover the poverty around their house or their business. It so often happens that the ambition to possess, while continuing to trample on rights, leads us to massacre human creatures and destroy whole families! It is so natural for the thirst for property to be without limits!

Happiness then becomes almost impossible. Neither material well-being, nor the satisfaction of every whim, nor the most refined comfort is lacking. But as the family is exposed to the danger of parallel homes, it risks, without a minimum of life in common, suffering from lack of love.

If providence thus places us in this environment, we are left with the difficult and delicate mission of breaking the shell, of melting the ice, of removing blinkers, of humanising and creating love.... And all this must be based on personal example and carried out with intelligence and tact, with humility and without arrogance, the overflowing hope of those who know that they are not alone, but servants of Jesus Christ.

What would the world become if christians, acting like this individually, were to unite for a collective action and bring hope back to the world of men!

Strange and curious hour! Our contemporaries have everything needed to make humanity completely happy. And yet, two-thirds, indeed over two-thirds of men are unhappy because of poverty; and the remainder are unhappy because of ambition, insensitivity, disquiet, anguish.

We christians are at the same time bearers of human weakness and sons of hope. Let us help our century to attack the root of despair. Let us denounce egoism as the cause of our material and moral despair, of our lack of hope, of the unhappiness which preys on the earth, of the fear whose shadow is gradually spreading over the world of men.

3. *Meeting our brothers who are victims of a lack of love*

After the discovery of coal, petroleum, electrical and

nuclear energy, will not man be able to go incomparably farther in the field of energy, when he finally learns how to tap and utilise love, which is 'the most universal, the most formidable, the most mysterious of the cosmic energies'? The lack of love is responsible for the unhappiness and the ignominy of the persistence of wars. And Vietnam proves this by demonstrating how, from day to day, war is becoming more senseless, more revolting and more amoral.

On the day when love becomes reality and when the dream of peace of the prophet Isaiah is accomplished —when swords are turned into ploughshares—what will we not be able to do with the astronomical sums now wasted on war?

The appeal made simultaneously to Khrushchev and to Kennedy has become famous: If each of them gave one bomber plane, the sum raised would maintain all the leper hospitals in the world for a whole year.

And now that the USA is planning its ABMS—the defence network against possible Chinese rockets— the sums set aside for this new Maginot Line would be sufficient to raise the whole of the Third World out of underdevelopment. It is impossible not to admire the daring and beauty of space travel, but it is a pity that the space race is so closely tied up with the arms race. If ambition and lack of love are truly the driving forces behind the present race to the stars, we do not deserve to leave the earth.

But why do I keep harping on these points, if all this only seems like a dream within a dream, fantasy within a fantasy! It is a dream and a fantasy because we christians are not committed to living in the fullness of love.

It is true that even if all the christian families were

united, we would still have war among the human race. But with us in this escalation of love, beyond christianity, and even independently of an explicit faith, there would be many anonymous christians, christians in acts, and men of good will.

And the most important thing is that we have Christ for us and with us, since he gave us the promise that there where two or three were gathered in his name, he would be among them. How could he fail to be with a revolution of love, conceived on a planetary scale by christians?

What would this explosion of love not be capable of if within human love there was divine love and if, in the human love bound to the lack of love, was present the spirit of love powerful, invincible and pure!

Appeal to christians of all denominations
The world is suffering from an undiagnosed need for faith, hope and love. Let us bring Christ to our atheist brothers marked by despair, who have even more need of living and true hope.

Let us bring Christ to our brothers who are victims of a lack of love, and they will be satisfied.

But it is not easy to bring Christ to others, and to bear him within oneself.

If God allowed Luther to reappear now and to speak to us, he would certainly say that to be worthy of Christ, to live the responsibility and joy of being a christian, to be able to help humanity in an effective way, the church would need, not only a Reformation, carried once and for all, but a permanent reformation, every day, every hour, every minute.

12
A prophet of development: Teilhard de Chardin

1965.

In honour of Pierre Teilhard de Chardin, in my strange Brazilian style, but with the whole body and soul of a man who has learned, with Teilhard, to view development in all its dimensions, I too bring you a cantata in six movements.

1st movement: A new vision of the world

For a great many christians, the world used to be the world for which Christ did not pray. The problem for men was to be in the world, to live in it, work in it, without belonging to the world.

There is a whole literature, very valuable no doubt on many counts, but based on the idea that the important thing was to pass as quickly as possible through life on earth with one's eyes firmly fixed on heaven. We need think only of the most famous Catholic religious book after the Gospel, *The Imitation of Christ*, in which we have all read the following: 'Every time I went out among men, I returned less man'.

There was in all this a great confusion. In practice,

it was not taken into account that the word 'world' in the Gospel has at least half a dozen meanings. And there was hardly ever an awareness that 'God so loved the world that he sent his beloved Son', Christ. Teilhard de Chardin has helped us to look at the world and to love it. It suffices to recall the unforgettable 'Mass on the world', which I hope one day Jolivet will transform into another cantata.

2nd movement: Man, co-creator

Very often, I meet timid people who ask me: 'Don't you think mankind is being incredibly daring? God isn't going to allow some frivolous man to split the atom with immunity, shoot to the stars like a god, sow new worlds.... One day imprudent man will start a fire in his own house and spark off the end of the world.'

This is the old idea of a jealous God, anxious not to be overtaken by man. As though the greatest joy of a father were not the glory of his son. The further the son goes, the happier the father.

On the day when man reaches what we imagine today to be the last of the stars, and then discovers other thousands of millions of worlds, he will be able to have a less poor, less miserable idea of God.

Thanks be to Chardin who teaches us to penetrate, fearlessly and joyfully, to *The Heart of Matter*.

3rd movement: Research, work and adoration

Sometimes, we believers are in danger of being unjust and hard on unbelievers who spend their lives in scientific research, without the solace of faith. And indeed, how many of them who consider themselves

132

atheists are only suffering from an unsatisfied theism?

And if these researchers devote themselves to their work in patience (it often means starting again from scratch dozens of times), in humility (very often with nothing to show for it), in loyalty (it is unthinkable to present as results what has not been rigorously tested), then these researchers, even if they consider themselves and call themselves atheists, are supported by God, led by his hand, enlivened by his breath!

Teilhard, help your brother researchers to discover that research, work and adoration are synonyms! Tell your brothers, the atheist scientists, your beautiful secret:

> I, for my part, am convinced that there is no more powerful natural food for the religious life than contact with scientific realities, well understood. . . . No one understands better than the modern man, dealing with matter, how Christ, through His Incarnation, is within the world, rooted in the world, to the heart of the smallest atom. . . .

4th movement: Beyond the blocs

Teilhard was no fool: he knew the distance between desire and capability; between having, and even knowing, and being. He knew suffering and the irreplaceable role of passivity and the humility of death. But he believed in human progress (we shall soon see what mission he reserves in this for Christ). He knew that humanity, for some two hundred thousand years or more, has not ceased to progress, move, as a whole in the direction of a higher cerebralisation and a close socialisation.

133

Given that the human brain, since *homo sapiens*, has more or less reached the absolute limit imposed by the corpuscular laws of matter on the complexity of an individual organic unit, it must be concluded that humanity must be going in the direction of socialisation.

And then, above the divisions into eastern and western blocs, beyond the distances created by egoism on a world scale, one can dream of a super-humanity, in the Teilhardian sense, of a human alliance whose sign will be a maximum of openness for the human person!...

5th movement: A vision of Christ for the space age
Teilhard de Chardin faced squarely not only the lesser problems of each of us but the great, the immense problems of humanity, of the world, of the universe.

He was not unaware of 'space sickness', i.e. the anguish of the man who is aware that he is lost in the starry wastes, nor the 'number sickness', the disturbing thought of everything that has been, of everything that is and everything that will be; the sickness of the unknown before us. . . . Nor the 'sickness of the impasse', i.e. the anguish of feeling caught up in the process of evolution, without knowing where it will lead. . . .

How many of our contemporaries, consciously or otherwise, fall into the pessimism which Chardin clearly foresaw! But he helps us to avoid it:

Either nature is closed to our demands for futurity, in which case thought, the fruit of millions of years of effort, is stifled, still-born in a self-abortive and absurd universe. Or else an opening exists—that of the super-soul above our souls. . . . [*The Phenomenon of Man*, London 1965, 256]

And Teilhard initiates us into the idea of the super-Christ.

But he warns us: 'By super-Christ I certainly do not mean *another* Christ, a second Christ, different from the first and greater than he; I mean the *same* Christ, the Christ of always, revealing himself to us in one figure and with dimensions, with an urgency and a surface of contact which are enlarged and renewed.'

And thus Teilhard opens our eyes, not to a private Christ, reduced to resolving our little personal problems, not to a mild Rabbi of Galilee, conventional, insipid, ridiculous, but to the true and only Christ whose mystery not even St Paul managed to gauge in all its length and breadth and height and depth.

Chardin proclaims to us the Christ of forever, so often distorted by our shrunken vision and swollen egoism. Christ the Alpha and Omega, the Beginning and End, whom the men of the space age, of interplanetary travel, will wish to adore. . . .

6th movement: Glory to Pierre Teilhard de Chardin
Pierre Teilhard de Chardin, although we are convinced that tomorrow we shall have super-humanity—especially given the fact that we have and shall have for all eternity the super-Christ—the fact is that we still have, in two-thirds of the world, men who resemble cacti more than the true human condition (dear Sister Smile, come to us and I will show you cactus flowers which have a face, a soul, a name!). We have, in two-

thirds of the world, sub-men without real homes, without real food or real clothing, without a minimum of education and working conditions. . . .

I have learned with you, Teilhard, to tremble with joy in seeing a man who has the courage to get out of a space capsule and remain suspended in space. . . . I am ready to salute landings on the planets. . . . But there is a price we must pay for going to the stars, and that is living on good terms with each other down here, on this tiny but remarkable earth. . . .

There should never be talk of super-production. It's a lie! It doesn't exist: there is, as everyone knows, sub-consumption by sub-men.

How happy I am to hear you talking of super-charity! But I am simply not quite sure that, for all men, charity is what it represents for us. I prefer to speak of super-love.

My brother men and my brother sub-men, my brother men and my brother angels, my sister earth and all of you, my sisters the stars, this evening let us perform a great dance of love and homage to the true super-man, who, inspired by the fire of the super-Christ, has taught men super-charity, super-love!